Make Your Own Chai, Mama's Boy!

Farah Tejani

Trafford rev. 09/19/2011

 www.trafford.com

North America & International
toll-free: 1 888 232 4444 (USA & Canada)
phone: 250 383 6864 ♦ fax: 812 355 4082

Acknowledgements

I would like to take this opportunity to thank my mother, Rashida Tejani, my aunt Laila , and my dear friends Barbara, Scott and Brian Graham for always believing in me and

refusing to let me give up.

I would also like to give special thanks to Jen Moss for providing me with excellent feedback

and a keen editor's eye.

And also to Keith Maillard, a great instructor who made a very big impact on me, now and forever.

I dedicate this book entirely to Rashida Tejani and Barbara Graham for

their endless support and patience. For hanging on to stories, that I had let go of,

and for patiently reading and re-reading through manuscripts.

I can honestly say, if not for them, this book would not be here today.

Table of Contents

The Cotton King

"Dama!" Chandan yells from the garden without looking up. "Bring us a cup of hot *masala chai!*" Chandan waves his empty cup in the air at Damayanti, who has already disappeared into the kitchen.

Us? She thinks to herself. Who's us? I don't even have a cup yet.

Damayanti walks around the bright yellow kitchen rummaging through the cupboards like a stranger in somebody else's home. She hates yellow. She will tell Chandan this. She will tell him she wants the kitchen to be red. Not bright red like the lipstick she must now wear for him everyday, as is his preference, but dull like the matte burgundy of blood after it has dried; rich burgundy sinks with chrome fixtures and alternating black and white floor tiles like the pictures she saw in an issue of Country Flair. Damayanti had dreamt of this kitchen many times before. But in her dreams she never shared it with a husband.

She looks up at the matching yellow lace curtains with embroidered white silk flowers. She reads the label on the back of the sash. *"Imported from London." They should be exported to the middle of the Indian Ocean. No, to the deepest part of the middle of the Indian Ocean, just so they don't float up and get washed up on some beach for someone to have to find—"*

"*Utapenda kunywa nini, Dama didi?*"

Damayanti turns to find the houseboy staring at her. He is wearing nothing but a thin cotton *lungi* that is wrapped tight around his waist. His chest is hairless and so are his cheeks. Dama had noticed his smooth black skin the first day Chandan introduced him to her. But she couldn't remember his name now. "Dama," Chandan had said, pointing his short, thick finger at the young black man, "this is Kziwa. He is hired especially for you, my Dama. He is completely at your disposing". It wasn't Chandan's weight, so much as his English that annoyed her.

"Chai? Dama *didi?*" The houseboy steps closer and leans over Damayanti to open the drawer under the oven. He pulls out a gadget that looks like a mini coffee bean grinder.

"No ... thank you ... Ka–Kali – Ka"

"Kziwa, madam ... I will prepare it myself for Raj Saheb."

"Yes. Thank you." This is new to her. She has never been a wife before, she has never had her own kitchen, and she has never had her very own Kziwa at her disposing. All she had was her mother... and her mother was too much everything. And here in Chandan's cotton castle, she is a lonely queen with too much nothing.

Kziwa hovers about the kitchen, while Damayanti watches him from the dining table. She watches the way he moves about without noise, as if being hunted and the slightest sound would give away his location. Kziwa hand-picks a select number of cinnamon splinters, cardamom, and cloves from each labelled jar in the yellow cupboard with the spinning tray. All the spice jars on the tray are the same size, with the same black-bordered label, with the same curly handwriting.

Damayanti wonders if this is the writing of the wife before her. She was an engineer, this is all she knows. And now she's not. Now she's dead but her memory lingers everywhere in Chandan's mansion, like the annoying smell of bleach that drifts over from his cotton factory next door.

Damayanti decides to look for old photos of the ex-wife. She will have to look hard because all the obvious ones of their marriage and the ones with their child will be burned. If there are any pictures of her, they will be solo shots, without Chandan—shots of her that he might have hidden somewhere. Damayanti knows she will be able to recognize her by the kitchen curtains she chose. Only a certain kind of woman is capable of that. She probably had an obsession with yellow saris, or two tone saris with ornate borders and busy prints, saris with all the wrong colors, side by side like silent enemies, held together by a neutral piece of silk that had no say in the matter. Damayanti knows that her hair would probably have been back-combed into an aggressive black beehive, not straight and plain like her own. Damayanti knows that she would have had highly picked brows and worn exaggerated make-up, matching her cream eye shadow with the boldest color on her sari.

And even if there are no pictures, she knows that in time she will come across love letters. Old love letters that she can hold up and compare to the curly writing on the spice jars when no one is around. What else can she do? She has asked if she can work in the cotton factory and come home at six in the evening with him, but he has said, "No vife of mine vill ever work. I vould be the laughing stock of Mombasa. Dama, they call me the King. Raj Saheb. Yes, really. They say, 'Namaste, Raj Saheb, aap kaise hai?' That's vhat they say. They come to me for help. They come to me for advice. My name is written on all the clothes these people wear. They call me King. And that makes you my Queen. And in the lives of a hundred sages, tell me Dama, how many Queens have you seen vorking?"

But maybe it's better this way. The less she sees him, the better chance that she might miss him one day. Tomorrow is Friday. Chandan comes after eight on Fridays. She will look for love letters then. She smiles.

"Why 'Kziwa'?" Her words break the silence that was so carefully created.

Kziwa looks around as if he has done something wrong. "Yes? Yes? I'm sorry, madam."

"No, no, Kziwa, no need for sorry. I am asking why Kziwa? Why the name? Kziwa."

Kziwa drops the spices into the grinder and presses power. When the grinding stops he turns and smiles with a mouthful of straight white teeth and says, "Pond ... Kziwa, yes. Kziwa mean a small pond."

"Pond." Damayanti says. "Oh."

Kziwa turns around. It is the first time he looks in her eyes since he came in the kitchen. "Why then they call you Dama, madam?"

"Actually, it's Damayanti."

Kziwa breaks it into syllables.

"Da-ma-yan-ti." He laughs. "Long."

"I was named after a King's daughter."

"Oh." Kziwa turns away and gets a silver tray from the cupboard, "you mean King like boss?"

"He's not really a king, Kziwa." Damayanti likes saying his name. Or maybe it's just the sound of her voice out loud. The only time she hears it is when she reads to herself or when she talks to her mother on the phone.

Damayanti starts to put the spice jars away.

"Yes, yes. Cotton King. He big Cotton King. See?" Kziwa undoes the tie piece of his *lungi*, the cotton sags and lowers in the front. Damayanti tries not to look and nods her head quickly as he shows her the white label against his smooth black skin: *"Sharma & Sharma."*

"Yes, I see," she says.

"Dama!" The voice comes again from outside. Only this time louder.

"Maybe better you go sit with Raj Saheb." Kziwa says while crushing the dry tea leaves into golden shreds in his palms. He waits for the pot to boil before he drops the leaves in. "I bringing it to you, Madam. I bringing it to you. No problem."

"His name is Chandan, you know?" Damayanti looks at him.

"Yes, I know. But I be working here for three years now and he never be telling me a calling him Chandan Saheb."

"Why?"

"He just say for me to be calling him Raj Saheb, and so I be—"

"Dama!" Chandan yells from outside. "What is the point of having very hot *chai* with very cold *chapati*. Already you are starting to sit on my head. What kind of situation has your mother gone and trapped me in?"

"Quick, quick. You must better go fast like. I will be bringing it to you, Madam, fast fast!"

Chandan sits in the shadow of the knotted baobab tree. He leans his heavy body to one side. One hand flat in the cool dry mud while the other grips a rolled *chapati* filled with a thick layer of butter and marmalade. A plate sits in front of him on a raised wooden stool. It is Thursday. Chandan's day off. Damayanti knows his Thursday ritual. Before the marriage was agreed to, Damayanti had to learn how to make perfectly saucer-shaped, paper-thin chapattis. A prerequisite for her employment as wife of cotton tycoon of Mombasa.

"Why are you yelling?" Damayanti asks her husband.

"Why are you taking such a long time? I am not asking you for *biriyani* or *ghos pilau!*"

It has only been three weeks now, and Damayanti has already figured him out. He likes to yell. He's not fond of much action after that. He just likes to yell.

"I should just ask Kziwa straight like. I put you in between and I soon die by thirst or starving." Chandan pinches her cheeks like a child's and smiles at the way they respond with color.

Damayanti walks back towards the white castle. She sits and watches him from the veranda. She is reading "The Collected Works of Robert Browning", her last text book from Nairobi Senior Secondary before she was shipped to meet her fate in Mombasa. It was her mother who had agreed to the proposal – partially because Chandan's parents were both killed early in his life, leaving no power figure for her to have to compete with, and partially because of Damayanti's inability to bear children, a great strike against her in the Matrimonials.

Her mother had left out this detail once, only to get bombarded with phone calls. Damayanti's picture was enough to attract the attention of all of the potential mother-in-laws. She met all the standard requirements. She was fair-skinned, slim, had straight long hair—a sign that the mother-in-laws learned to interpret as submission. It was assumed that women who styled their own hair had a mind of their own and might be a force to be reckoned with. She had straight teeth, no facial scars, and a high forehead which stood for respectability and purity. She even had a beauty mark just below her left eye.

Damayanti's mother had had the picture taken with a professional photographer from Nairobi. The picture was a flawless shot of Damayanti leaning on a mirror table. She held her face in her hand and looked devoutly at the camera while her other hand held a rose. The photographer was indeed a professional. He knew the look required for successful matrimonial shots. He even had a framed wall piece that mentioned the names of all the women who were successfully married because of his professional photography. A sign outside his small shop read: "I can even make the bad look good!"

Behind the camera was a large screen. He had slides of all the gods. You could choose. Ganesh, Shiva, Christ, Guru Nanak... Even Damayanti was impressed when the picture arrived in the mail. She was a mountain of beauty; one that the mirrored table reflected into itself like a sea. Damayanti's mother had paid 5000 shillings extra for an original pose. An agreement was then signed between the photographer and her. None of the other pictures in the Matrimonials would use a mirror table with a red rose. Agreed.

Most of the other pictures in the Matrimonial ads were straight headshots or full length shots, without the frills. This picture suggested more than just a fine photographer. It suggested wealth.

And wealth suggested dowry. But the one thing that Damayanti's mother had not thought the picture would suggest was desperation. The mother-in-laws were smart. Damayanti was too beautiful for the Matrimonials. Suitors should flock to her on the streets. She, herself, should be her own advertising. They knew that there had to be some catch. Most of them asked questions like: "Does she have polio?", "Is she paralyzed?", "Is she thigh heavy?", "Does she have burn scars on her legs?", "Is she missing any of her toes or limbs?"

Then one day, one of them came right out and asked, "What's wrong with her bottom half?" But it wasn't too long before one of them finally asked the right question, "Can she have children?" It was then that mother changed the ad in the Nairobi Connection:

Damayanti Ramesh Chowdry:

17 years old, 52 kilos, tall and fair,

beautifully attractive and educated to the senior level Nairobi High School- Specialty in English, never before married. Pure, untouched, unable to bear children, perfect health condition, with no scars, birthmarks or disease. Cooking and Cleaning, very easily trainable and very domestic respectable good girl.

The only part she lied about was her height, her weight, and her cooking abilities. Which is not bad considering the last ad. Damayanti is not incredibly tall at 5'1", and she's 41 kilos, not quite as plump and healthy as the ad suggests. She is attractive, no doubt, but she can barely manage to cook an egg without burning it. But when Chandan first laid eyes on her he was enchanted by her beauty. When he lifted the sari from her face in order to make his final approval (a nod to Damayanti's mother), it was her beauty that took him over. She was as fair as her name had implied. Damayanti, daughter of King Bhima, ruler of Vidarbha. One with the fairest complexion and the slimmest waist. Her palace, surrounded by hundreds of female slaves, and her charm ensnared all who came across it.

They say even the moon lost its course in the sky due to her looks. Though her name stood out in the Matrimonials, no mother was ever bold enough to name a daughter after one of the fairest legendary Princesses in all of time. No mother except Damayanti's of course. While other mothers hid within the superstition that all forms of vanity will surely lead to doom and misfortune, Damayanti's mother believed that vanity was hers by right.

Dama looks at the open book in her hands. The words are there, the very same words that took her far away into dreams of her future:

"... The sullen wind was soon awake,
It tore the elm tops down for spite ..." *

But now they are just words. And looking at the acres of land that spread past Chandan, sitting in a veranda, with white wicker chairs, she is far from her dreams.

In the middle of this private flower garden trimmed with jasmine trees hedged in with trimmed bushes, living in a mansion with more furniture than she has time to sit in—furniture that she never played a part in choosing, walking through halls with more black servants than guests—Dama knows she is a stranger. A stranger in somebody else's dream.

---

*   Robert Browning, "The Collected Works of Browning",
    Porphyria's Lover

She looks up from her book at Chandan. The oven-like sun has made his skin stick to the cotton of his *shalvar.* It is supposed to fit loosely, but not even the largest size can fall loosely around his expanded stomach.

"But he is fair." Damayanti's mother had said after Chandan left the house following the nod of approval. Damayanti looks at Chandan by the tree. Yes, he is fair. Damayanti thinks to herself. He's old enough to be her father, he's fat like a balloon, he walks like he has to go to the bathroom, but he is fair.

"There is no question to be even thought of," Damayanti's mother had come all the way to school and snatched her from her class to bear the news to her. "He is a little bit heavy, you know, but you are also a bit too skinny, right? His name is Chandan Mehta Sharma, and he is having only one small baby son, very easy to take care, but this is nothing to worry because, you see, he is a big, big businessman, owner of the Sharma Cotton Estate, with big, big white house, almost as big as the cotton factory! Well, it is in Mombasa, but I will visit. So, hurry now, and stop looking at me like this. For God's sake Dama, there will be no other proposals, I am telling you. You should thank the most gracious gods that they are feeling pity on you. You are too old and time is not to be doing you any favours anymore. So come now quickly, because there is still many, many things to be taken care of. Fast, fast."

Damayanti did not return to class that afternoon. Four days later, when her teacher finally phoned, the call lasted only three minutes. Damayanti's mother had spoken in a matter of fact way, and there seemed to be no objections on the other end.

"Dama!"

Damayanti places her book on the table and looks towards her new husband.

"Dama," he says with a big smile that she can see from where she is standing. "Come and read your precious book to me. You must make me as smart as you. I cannot have such a lovely bride attempt to outdo my vits.

What wits? Damayanti thinks to herself while she walks towards him. Damayanti knows that he will want to touch her breasts while she reads to him. She knows that he will be overcome with passion and will want to make love to her right there. She knows that he has probably made love to his precious wife at this same spot, by this same tree, with this same taste of *masala chai* and marmalade on his lips. But Damayanti also knows that this man's home will be the only home she will ever come to know outside of the wretched home her mother created for her after her father's death.

Chandan lifts himself up to meet her when she draws near, a formality that Damayanti knows will soon wear down in time. She imagines growing old with this man standing before her. She imagines growing old with him, with his factory, with his big, big home, with his son – but what she cannot imagine growing old with is herself.

Chandan reaches for her book and places it down by the chapatti stool. He rises slowly with his hands on either side of her slim girlish body. Her breasts are not fully developed yet, but Chandan seems excited by this. He grips at them and fondles them, like the chapatti dough that Damayanti learned to knead and press for him. Chandan kisses her softly on her lips. He moves his head from side to side like the Indian film stars in the movies. When he kisses her,

Damayanti closes her eyes and imagines different men. All kinds of men. Men she has never known... sometimes not even Indian men.

The day before when Chandan pressed against her at night, she secretly dreamt of a tall, white man with long brown hair that he tied back in a pony tail. He was slim, maybe even too slim, but he never wore Sharma cotton. Even on hot days he wore suits. Silk suits like actors. Slight colours: gray, khaki, beige, olive. He brought cheap flowers for her. He set them on her bed. He fondled her passionately and caressed her in sweet places. He didn't notice that she was still a girl. To him, she was his lover. He pressed hard against her, and it was in this hard that she felt a kind of safety. Even a kind of power.

Chandan pulls her down slowly. He beckons her to lean against the tree. But he doesn't have to, this is the third Thursday and Damayanti has already learned her duties. Except for one of course. Damayanti is still a virgin. It is in this that she feels she has to respect Chandan. He did not push her on her wedding night. And when the legendary phone call came from the mother of the bride, to subtly allude to the success or failure of the night of penetration, Chandan had merely said, "All is well, mother. The house is joyful with the gift you have shared with me". And he smiled and pinched Damayanti's cheek softly.

Chandan rests his head in Damayanti's lap and asks her to read while he watches her lips move to form the words. She knows that Chandan is in love with her English. She will stare into the fine print and pretend as if she is reading, but the words are already memorized because she always reads him the same poem by Robert Browning—though he never notices:

"... The rain set early in tonight,

12

The sullen wind was soon awake,
It tore the elm tops down for spite,
And did its worst to vex the lake,
I listened with heart fit to break,
When glided in Porphyria straight,
She shut the cold out and the storm,
And kneeled and made the cheerless grate,
Blaze up and all the cottage warm ..." *

Chandan turns slowly to his side and with one hand firmly grips Damayanti's thigh. He never needs more than a verse or two to get excited. But Damayanti keeps reading. He does not notice as she looks up from the book and reads to the sky and the tree beyond. She feels his hand under her think silk sari, and when it touches her skin she closes her eyes and puts her book down. She wraps herself in a cloak of darkness. A safe nothingness. She repeats the empty phrases in her head until they lead her to a dream. She reaches deep inside to try and make out the details. First they are blurry, but as she struggles to focus, the image sets in. Today, Chandan's hands belong to a simple but handsome Indian street builder. He is poor, as his simple cotton *lungi* indicates, but not too poor to shave. His jaw is square set and his body is not as weak as it appears. His hands are dry and calloused, but his touch is soft and subtle. Damayanti treasures each movement, each impulse. The man's hand traces her breasts without touching them, and follows the soft curve of the back of her neck. Damayanti leans back into his hand, and he supports her gracefully. He plays with her untied hair, running his fingers through her freshly washed curls releasing the sweet smell of rosewood scented oil. He guides her head down and

---

*   Robert Browning, "The Collected Works of Browning", _
     Porphyria's Lover

13

lies on the ground beside her. He fondles her breasts through her sari blouse. Her nipples respond to his delicate touch. Damayanti moves closer to him and melts into the rhythm of his fingers. He kisses her neck and presses into the warmth of her body. When he unties the string of her slip, the sari falls into a loose puddle of silk around her waist. His fingers inch slowly up her thighs, pressing and –A baby cries in the distance.

Dama opens her eyes and sits straight up, "Raju is crying, he must be hungry."

Chandan looks at her strangely, "Kziwa vill take care of him, that's vhy I hired him. Vhy are you vorrying?"

Damayanti pictures this little baby she has only known for three weeks, rescuing her with his cries; as if somehow knowing. She pictures him in his sky blue room with a view of the open fields that he doesn't know how to appreciate. He could learn how to walk in that room and still never explore the same spot twice. He could even learn how to run in that room if he likes.

"Kziwa is a houseboy, what does he know about babies?"

"Kziwa has three of his own, Dama." Chandan reaches softly towards her, "Please, Dama. I only vant to love you. I am good, you vill see. I am gentle. I von't hurt you."

"Did you hurt your last wife?"

"Dama! Please. You must only talk on things your business. This thing is not your business!"

Chandan looks hurt by this and somehow this makes him just a little more human. Damayanti looks up at the house toward the soft singing of Kziwa. She looks up at the baby's window and imagines Kziwa holding a child like it were his own – wishing he could be with his own. How he must wait for the weekends.

"Maybe Kziwa's children can come and stay one night a week, there are so many rooms. And don't say that the other servants will start demanding things, because they won't. He is a live-in. He makes sacrifices. He has a right to some privileges, doesn't he, Chandan?" Damayanti feels odd saying his name, she never ever seems to have the chance to use it, and looks at Chandan who has his eyes closed. Chandan puts his arms around Damayanti and pats her thigh.

"You are as smart as the River Knowledge itself. Come. You are as sweet as any prize worth vaiting for. I will vait. And tomorrow, I vill arrange for the children to be brought to the house. It vill be a surprise. It is a good thought, Dama. It is a good thought." Chandan places his hand on Damayanti's and leans back down to the ground. He undoes his pant-string, and rubs against Damayanti's bare stomach. Damayanti cannot close her eyes. She cannot dream with his weight shifting above her, and his groans loud in her ears. She can do nothing but stare up at the tree and listen to Raju's cries for his real mother's milk. Chandan's rhythm quickens and his breath turn into grunts in her ear. Chandan rolls onto his back and lies beside Damayanti.

"You know, Damayanti, just smelling you I am excited," he says to her.

Damayanti closes her eyes and braces herself as the wind brushes cold over the liquid on her blouse and stomach. Chandan lies there for a moment, breathing heavily. In the pause between his breaths Damayanti hears a noise. She looks up at the window next to the baby's room. Looking closer, she catches an image. Kziwa. She stays still. Exposed. Turning to Chandan, she sees that his eyes are closed.

Looking up, Damayanti slowly undoes her sari blouse. Her eyes meet Kziwa's and a passion burns inside her. He does not move from the window. She knows he will not. When the sun rests on her bare chest, she turns to Chandan.

"I am ready," she says.

Seven Stones

"When I bring to you coloured toys my child, I understand why there is such a play of colours on clouds, on water, and why flowers are painted in tints... when I give coloured toys to you my child."

When I bring sweet things to your greedy hands. I know there is honey in the cup of the flower and why fruits are filled with sweet juice... when I bring sweet things to your greedy hands." *

Deep in the heart of the mango grove sat Maburu, not everyone's Maburu, but mine. It took me years to find him—but I did. Maburu's guise was that of an old man made of the softest wood carved into the bark of one of the trees; a spirit guide, perhaps even my conscience. His face set in motion the memory of an old song I remember from years back. A song my mother sang to the moon.

Five years back on a stretch of ploughed land lay a small bird with shattered wings. I called this bird "Desire" and set it on its way. The repairing took three days, and when "Desire" sprang forth into

* Rabindranath Tagore, Gitanjali

17

the sky with a gentle burst from my cradling arms, I somehow knew what was to follow. For the same three and a half days I went back to the same field hoping to find another damaged bird. But all I found was myself looking for a way out. Maburu tells me this later—too many years later for it to matter anymore.

Ilahi was my first-born and last to this day. He came out of me like a full-grown man with a calling of sorts and I wept fourteen hours for him to surge. Feet first of course, kicking and screaming like the air was no good... But the air was good—it was just the place that wasn't. You'd think I'd know to go back to the same mango tree where I bore Ilahi to find Maburu. But I didn't. And that is why it took so long. In the dead of the night it dawned on me in a silence I did not prefer. And in this night I travelled only to find this soft wooden spirit with a message I had already foreseen.

Ilahi burst forth much like the bird I had saved years before. Ilahi poured out of me onto the grass like a big red stain and I feared that I had miscarried. Not a soul heard me screaming in the thick of the trees because the bulbuls screamed far louder than my cries. Ilahi was born at the crack of dawn when the birds owned the sky and the people owned their slumber. I knew his name long before he emerged so I called out to him while searching through the still warm mess between my thighs. It was our cord that I got hold of first and so I drew him out of me like water from a well. Ilahi slid up my body with no more weight than a handful of small mangos. I squeezed the cord and wrestled with his tongue. Even the bulbuls had to stop and listen. With his eyes pinched closed he screamed into the day like fire in a dry forest. Why he screamed was always a mystery to me, but Maburu said he was never mine. Ilahi screamed for a way back in—while I looked for a way out.

The first gift from his father was a painted coconut with yellow feathers. Though it stood beyond me what a three-day old was to do with such a gift, I flashed it before him long before his eyes could see. It made no difference to Ilahi, but I did it just the same. His eyes still grey with ignorance looked off into the distance never catching a hold of the coconut's path. The feathers had matted with the heat of the reef packaging it had been sent in, and the powder paint would come off where my fingers held it. And although I know it was not his father's hand that had created such a thing it was if he did just by packaging it.

The box had simply read: "Jaya Asman, 14 Adhuri Gate". I looked for a note or a return address, but he had left the village at the first sign of my swelling stomach. I imagined him counting the months to nine, or a figure close to nine anyway. And how the gift arrived exactly three days after his birth warmed my heart like the smell of Ilahi's soft brown skin in the sun. Somehow he knew he had bore a child in another place from another time. And this was all that really mattered. I folded the paper packaging with his father's penmanship and buried it at the foot of the tree as proof to Ilahi and I—for I knew the day would surely come when he would ask. (Or at least I had hoped this day would come).

Ilahi's father first saw me through the window of my home. He had come on his bike delivering medication from the local druggist to my mother. She took the package from his hands but must have watched how his eyes searched beyond hers to my bedroom window. I know this is what she must have done.

I peered from behind the curtain, naked—though he could not tell, and found my hand touching myself gently as he rode away. I wanted to show this man my soft brown skin. A passion inside me flared like a match on fresh petrol and I wanted to just tell this strange man how I longed for our shades of skin to touch. Just then, as if hearing my words, he looked up. My mother called from below, "Away from the windows, Jaya. A black man is near." But away I could not stay, and didn't.

Four days after Ilahi was born, I returned to the village as I was growing tired of eating mangoes and my milk was running thin. My breasts ached; Ilahi pulled at them so fiercely with his strong toothless gums and I knew then the first signs of a grudge he bore against me. The stain in the grass began to smell of fear so I turned to my village with a dignity in my stride I had never noticed before. With Ilahi now bathed and cleaned by the fresh stream at the foot of the mango tree I did not fear my welcoming until I arrived at the gate. It was Edna that I saw first. And Edna I saw last. She screamed my name in a way of warning as opposed to joy. I do not remember if it was my father or my mother that had come out first, but it was no matter, because the villagers had already gathered around the house as if to prevent me from seeing.

Ilahi howled at the rumblings of the crowd that had gathered as if cursing each foreign voice he registered. One bulbul cried loudly before the first stone was thrown, and in a flurry of terror I began to run back in the direction I had come. Looking back one last time, I caught Edna's face. It was her arm cutting through the air! It was her stone! The other stones that followed hers did not reach us, but I heard them falling behind like heavy rain. And it was mother's voice that shouted, "Come back alone or not at all!" and father's that screamed, "No daughter of mine would ever—". But the words faded into my grunts and Ilahi's cries, and I knew them anyway.

In one last look back I searched the crowd for the one that had come and delivered the coconut—for it had to be one of them. But there was not one smile amidst the jumbled scowls. And then her face came back to me, and in its tender creases I knew it must have been Edna. She must have stole away in the night. She must have held Ilahi in her arms and shed tears on his face, searching it for features that resembled mine. She must have touched his cool half-breed skin with a love of indifference that I knew only too well. And really, what could she do but cast the first stone? Cast the first stone in an act of warning or validate my crime.

It was, after all, a very small stone she chose.

I had pledged to count the days with stones around the tree and only got to seven.

Seven stones.

Seven stones and a painted coconut with only one yellow feather left. Shattered like Desire's—well, those are Maburu's words of course. I did not—I could not know then what I know now. Maburu's wisdom was not of this world.

I pledged to count the days with stones around the tree—days to months to years. It would only be a dozen years before he would charge back into the village—a man with a mission of sorts. And a dozen years meant a stone garden around his birthing tree. How else could I tell him his age—or mine for that matter?

I pledged to count the days with stones around his birthing tree—and with each stone, a new prayer and a new feature to notice on his fast aging face. And, oh, how many faces he made, and yet in all of them, not one like his father's.

Yes. I pledged to count the days with stones.

But the seventh one was his last...

I lay with Ilahi two days after seven. It was all I could bare. His body was puffed out and as swollen as the stomach that bore him and his skin began to smell with the heat from the indignant sun.

With one hand I had held him under. Ilahi simply breathed in the water like air. And though his eyelids closed it was this he couldn't do for me. I felt them open beneath my fingers. These same eyes that looked into the distance at his father's gift, pierced straight through me. And the stream, it was clear as glass. Small fragile bubbles from his nose and mouth came to the surface with little or no sound. And if he struggled or not, I cannot remember. I will not remember. And even the bulbuls, too, stayed silent this morning—perhaps praying, perhaps cursing.

When his fists uncurled from what little fight he put up, his eyes released their hold on me and rolled to the back of his head—white to the sky. With one sweeping motion, I shrieked and clutched his cold body to my breasts, and as the icy water ran down my sides I saw flashes of anger and passion and pictures of faces I had known and things I had done. I saw: Edna's face, Ilahi's father slipping into me like the night, mother's piercing eyes, father's hand firmly gripping my throat, Ilahi's bubbles surfacing and white eyes, now no more ignorant as they once were grey, but instead filled with a knowledge of things well beyond this realm. I begged for him to come back, but he would not listen. He lay in my arms limp and still, and all the while I knew his feathers had been repaired.

I kicked the coconut into the stream and watched the powdered paint float to the surface like coloured milk—and why the feather did not float to the surface I will never know. I did not turn back. I pictured it wedged between the coconut and the earth, torn and weathered by the stream – fighting to fly.

Maburu's mission served he faded back into the tree. My Maburu. My conscience. And as his soft wrinkles merged back into the pattern of the bark, I believe I heard him faintly singing a song I know only too well. Only it was not until after he was fully merged back into Ilahi's birthing tree that I knew it to be my mother's song to the moon:

> "If the day shall come, if birds sing no more,
> Take me to rest on your Ever-Loving Shore.
> But if night begins, and new sounds take flight,
> Let me but stay through...
> One more wretched night."

Curried Tuna

Raju Creighton stared at the blank notebook in front of him and then set his pen in motion. He always wrote first and then typed it in later:

DEAR LOOKING FOR MISS KAMA SUTRA QUEEN,

There is no such thing. Get the fuck out of your situation, get to your nearest Convenience Store, pick up a trashy magazine, and be done with it. Any way you slice it, the bird you're with ain't gonna get any better. How does that saying go? A bird in the mind is always better than the one underneath you? Yeah, something like that...

Sincerely,
Curried Tuna

Raju worked for Pak Attack - the most alternative South Asian Rag in all of East Van. Only a few knew about it. Better to keep a steady following than to disturb the masses.

Raju put his pen down, crumpled the piece of paper and tossed it over his shoulder into a pile of several others just like it.

Curried Tuna.

This was the pen name he chose for himself when he was first hired two and a half years ago. The editor hired him over a brief and somewhat peculiar on-line interview. To this day he has never formally met his boss, Kuldeep Grewal, but has seen him at many of the gay bars in Vancouver. Raju had filled out an application to work for the Pak Attack, and received a response via messenger while checking his email just three days later:

Kuldeep: Hey, Raju, you're online...got a moment?
Raju: Sure... who are you?
Kuldeep: Kuldeep Grewal, Editor, Pak Attack.
Raju: Right... You received my application.
Kuldeep: Indeed... Just have a few q's.
Raju: Shoot.
Kuldeep: You are South Asian?
Raju: Yup.
Kuldeep: Are you gay?

Raju seemed surprised but without missing a beat typed in:

"Well, that depends, Mr. Grewal. How much money do you make a year and can you send me your picture?" Kuldeep responded with "LMAO, Mr. Creighton—so far, so good...next question. How would you like to contribute to The Pak Attack"?

Raju had typed in: "Well, I was thinking perhaps an advice column for South Asians to address issues of clashing cultural concerns or problematic relationships such as homosexuality, arranged marriages, marrying into another culture or faith and other such quandaries."

"So, what you're saying is an Anne Landers/Dr. Ruth type advice column?"

"No...I was thinking more along the lines of an Anne Slanders/Dr. Truth, hard-line, say it like it is, slap-in-the-face, column by like say a columnist... like me. You know... Amitaabh Bachaan meets Shah Rukh Khan in the London Underground—no holds barred, no stuntmen."

"I see. Very interesting, and do you want it to be called "Ask Raju Vreighton?"

"It's Creighton—but no names... I'd prefer it to be anonymous... maybe call it...Curried Tuna... just a pen name."

"Done. I like that. The magazine will be announcing this new addition to its readers by next month's issue...get ready...what is it you are expecting for pay?"

"By the hour or set salary...it really doesn't matter."

"Agreed...we'll see how the readers respond. And did you want to send in a photo."

"No names. No pictures... I'd prefer it to be anonymous, sir."

"Fine. No reason for formalities, Raju. Let the games begin."

And that was that. The readers responded and so did he. The pay was more than he had hoped for and it sure beat his last job at The Courier managing ads and mundane articles, bouncing here and there as a gopher, going for this person's doughnuts and that person's chili from Horton's.

Raju looked up at the clock in the kitchen. Twelve fifty-nine. It was stuck. He looked at the throw rug on the floor, worn and frayed, and wondered to himself where this job might take him.

Dear Looking For Miss Kama Sutra Queen (Take Two),

Let's just face it. We all want Aishwarya Rai, or Priyanka Chopra, or a combo pack of them both - but those are all big screen names and most likely, even bigger OFF SCREEN BITCHES. Settle for what fate throws you... You'll be better off,

> Sincerely,
> Curried Tuna

P.S. the Kama Sutra's overrated. Try "Love Toys and Love Joys" by Me.

"Enough of this," Raju muttered to himself. He went into his bedroom and got his denim jacket off the bed and went back to the computer. A one-bedroom studio, he pretty much had four choices: Sleep, Shit, Eat or Write. He reached for the last drag of his smoke, but it had already steadily burned away leaving only a long thin skeleton of ashes. He lit another and headed out the door leaving the computer softly humming in time with the fridge.

He swung open his apartment door to East Broadway. A steady blur of colours whizzed by before his eyes. He took a drag, put on his jacket and then yielded into the people of the night.

The fight was on. Tyson and Lewis—something to steady his mind. He glanced down Main Street. In the distance he saw that some stood in line-ups at local pubs, while others seemed not to care whatsoever. To be honest, he was one of the latter. Fights were never his thing, but with half a stale beer in the fridge and just stale Cheetos and dry cereals to munch on, somehow the option seemed worthy of serious consideration.

While standing in line at the Unicorn Tree, Raju looked himself over. What he enjoyed most about his shitty job was that he never had to dress a certain way for anybody. They hired him for his words. Raju dressed for no one. Today, he was in a pair of fitted black rustic jeans, a white t-shirt that read, "Don't read this!" with a bunch of tiny letters underneath that read, "I said, don't!" and a dark denim jacket his partner had given him before the car accident. This day, Raju wanted to remember.

The line up began to dwindle, but there were still another five or six people ahead of him. He thought about what his mother had said to him two weeks ago. "Let go of this notion that you are dipperent. If you keep saying you are dipperent, you vill become dipperent by depault, and then it is your own pault. Try to do normal things. Vy make jore lipe so dippicult, Raju? Just look at me and jore dad." Mother had an idea, but never came out and said anything directly. "This priendship thing with Anil vas an ill omen and the sooner you porget it the better." His mother was a strict Punjabi widow who had married a far more liberal British man—which left Raju in the middle—a bit of both. *Curried Tuna*. Raju likes to believe his father would have been way more accepting. For the fourteen years he knew his father, he had learned this much for sure: Honesty, first and foremost, and to thine own self be true. His dad used to say, "Whatever you do son, make sure you do it with passion and because you want to. You will never be happy until you are true to who you are." And he would point at his son's chest. "It's got to feel good in here. For you."

The average age of the people at the pub he had chosen was nineteen to around twenty-five, he guessed. And at thirty-four with an identity crisis, he just didn't cut it at the Unicorn, unless he was on some kind of mind-altering substance. Even though he might have been able to solve that situation in a matter of minutes, Raju didn't want to be buzzed this day. He decided to lose his place in line and go a few blocks further to The Rusty Nail whether the fight was showing or not.

Raju flicked his smoke and walked up the street. The wind blew through his hair and whistled for him to listen. His eyes caught the eyes of a woman walking towards him. The wind pushed her from behind, forcing her to walk faster. She clutched at her handbag and shifted a plastic Safeway bag of vegetables to her other hand. Raju searched his mind for something to say. Something. Anything.

"Excuse me, could you tell me the time?"

How original, he thought. Could have just said, "Hey."

The woman slowed down a bit and stared at him blankly and then continued walking faster than she was before. He had noticed the green onions, which led him to notice her wrist, which led him to notice her watch. He knew the time. It was twenty minutes into the fight. He had just wanted to give this normal thing a try.

He looked back to see if she might turn to see him. But she had already disappeared. Probably ducked and hid in some apartment lobby. Did he really look that scary? All men must look scary to women. Superman is dead and all the other action heroes are too busy fighting crime to care about courtship. He thought about the advice he had given a woman who had complained of enduring great lengths of emotional abuse due to your average string of Indian men.

Dear Miss I Have Had It With All East Indian Men,

I wish I could empathize with your situation but I'm afraid you have no grounds. All men and women suck equally, and looking for some kind of everlasting Zen happiness is like eating a rose and expecting it to taste good. Just try to remember two things: I, too, have had it with all East Indian women, and horse manure with dill pickles is always better than getting your dog stuffed by a taxidermist.

Sincerely,
Curried Tuna

Really speaking, his was a cushy job. Apparently, according to his boss, Grewal said the mag had picked up quite a few readers with many of them writing in to his column for his candour and wit. Really speaking, to get paid to throw words together in some kind of grumpy salad with a slap in your face dressing was right up his alley. Growing up as a young boy in Manchester he would get the shit kicked out of him for this kind of lip. And who'd have thought, years later it would be what paid the bills. Easy. He gave them what they wanted. The Pak Attack was just that. An attack against the Pak; but mostly a rag for the Indian fag. A rarity, indeed. Or so he thought.

Inside, he watched a greasy old man throwing his fist at the TV.

"Just another drunkard in a pub," he muttered to the bartender.

"Well, I'm just another floozy in the bar." Floozy introduced herself with a drunken handshake. "So, what do you do?"

Raju always had prepared an absurd, yet, well-accepted answer, that if said with just the right eye contact, speed and intonation would undoubtedly put to rest even the most inquisitive mind.

"Oh, just a variety of multi-faceted tasks that involve cubicles and letters."

He found that by throwing in the word "cubicles" he was less likely to get more questions after that.

Just then the people in the Pub booed. Tyson was still not down. Finally, the same drunk yelled back over the noise: "Ahh! What do you know? The longer the fight goes, the more the fame in losing."

Raju was mildly impressed by this bar-side profundity.

"So? You want to leave or what?" Raju asked Floozy, boldly.

"Sure," she slurred. "I've been waiting for you to say that."

They walked up the street to the Biltmore. Raju let Floozy press her drunken weight on him. Hand in hand, he motioned for the key. This was not new to the desk clerk. She passed him a key with a plastic red cat on it that said "204". Raju nodded and said, "Just an hour." He wasn't even remotely embarrassed when the two women at the elevator turned to see the face that came with the words. He turned and caught a look at himself in the hall mirror. Both subdued and stunned he guided Floozy to the far elevator and led her to the room

Floozy asked if she could bum a smoke. Raju pulled out a folded American five-dollar bill and set it on the bed. He pulled out a pipe from his jacket pocket and Floozy warned, "but, what about the smell?" He wanted to say, "Hey lady, I'd be more worried about the booze on your breath", but instead he said, "It's not like we're smoking pot, we're just free-basing cocaine." Floozy picked something out of her hair and flicked it at him.

Raju exhaled a stream of thick smoke towards Floozy's lips. She inhaled and took it all in. She began to take her yellow and white halter top off, and then she moved over to the bed, pulling the straps up again. "Can we order something first, I've only had a couple of slices of toast."

"Certainly." Raju said stone-faced. He picked up the phone and ordered Anil's favourite: "Yes, we'll have some Angels on Horseback, please."

"What's that?" Floozy reached for the pipe.

"It's just some fish wrapped in bacon." He already knew that the hotel didn't carry scallops. "Alright then, we'll have some poutine."

Raju took in some more velvety smoke, reminding himself that he had not wanted to be high this night. This day last year he lost Anil. But what could he do? It was his fault. Anil had said he didn't want to go to the film, but Raju insisted. A little tipsy, and high on ecstasy, Raju crashed head-first into an oncoming car. Raju made it. Anil wasn't belted.

"It's so cool, isn't it... I mean the way we met because I sure don't know..." Raju let Floozy's words blend into the street noise. It didn't matter. He thought about the advice he would give himself if he wrote in to the Pak Attack.

DEAR MAN WITHOUT A MISSION,

Get off the cross, somebody else needs the wood. The sooner you realize that you have no purpose, the better off you will be. When is the last time you saw a wart-ridden frog marry a successful female architect. That in itself, should put things into perspective. Fags are fags like pigs will eat anything. Wear it with some pride you dumb ass. It's fags like you that make the real ones look flippant. Suck it up, shithead, and give Springer a call.

Sincerely,
Curried Tuna

Floozy stopped talking and moved in closer. Raju watched as she began to slowly dance in front of him taking off what little she had on. Raju pictured touching her uneven sagging breasts with his hands, his lips, his.... Oh, not today, he thought to himself, life is like farting and shitting yourself instead. Anil would have liked that one.

Raju stopped Floozy before she could untie her sarong. He pulled some crumpled bills out of his back pocket and placed them on the end table, and walked towards the cracking orange door. "Here's the money for the food," he said, "I've got to go."

Floozy held her halter-top over her breasts and looked genuinely concerned. "Did I do something wrong?"

Raju picked up the key from the end table and threw Floozy what was left of his pack of smokes. Floozy missed the catch and they bounced on the bed. She shrugged and pulled a cigarette from the pack and said, "Well, I hope we get to see each other again."

"But of course." Raju painted on a mechanical grin. "I haven't had this much fun since I put that ground beef in my milk bottle."

"Really? Wow...cool!"

Floozy flopped down on the bed. Raju shook his head and chuckled at how his response had somehow soothed her. He closed the door on a normal thing he would vow to forget by the time his head hit his pillow.

An Indian Thing

Spinster's eyes are always on me. "Slowly, *beti*, slowly". I slurp the remainder of the soup and lick my spoon.

"It will be most difficult to find a tall, fair, man of good upbringing, if you, yourself, are not." Spinster talks with her right hand. A flat palm, cutting and slicing the air. An Indian thing.

"Why does he have to be fair-skinned? He could be the whitest Indian and a part time serial killer and you would still pick him over a dark man!" I yell after her shadow on the wall.

Silence. I flick the T.V. on.

"No T.V., no phone, no outings! You know what your father said, so you don't play any smart, smart games with me, do you hear?" Her voice comes out of her locked bedroom.

The next morning the living room phone, the TV remote, and the bathroom latch lock are missing. I try to picture Spinster unscrewing the bathroom latch.

"I'm not staying in this hell hole."

"I do not think this is your choice." Spinster replies calmly from the other side of her bedroom door.

"You can't keep me like this. My dad didn't say lock me up like some criminal and hide the phones! I need privacy when I go to the bathroom!" I punch her door hard.

I can hear Spinster moving in her room and walking towards the door. I imagine her with a bat in her hand or a hanger. But Spinster has nothing. She opens the door wide, and with one hand leaning against the door, the other hand cuts and chops at my face. "If you are paying mortgage here, then you can hit the walls. Okay?" She is not smiling.

"Okay," I retreat.

Spinster closes the door and ends the discussion in one move.

I am sentenced to the Spinster's for one month. A lot of young girls in our community have been sentenced to the Spinster's, but they always come out looking worse than when they went in.

Shashi was sentenced to her for the time that she got caught sticking gum in the portable's door lock. It was in November, and the whole class had to wait outside, in minus eleven degrees, for almost all of first block, so that the janitor could melt the frozen gum with a soldering iron, and then pick it out, in little pink bits, with a paper clip. Shashi got a week for that.

Bina had to stay with the Spinster for three and a half months, until school got out for the summer. She was six months and starting to show. Her parents wanted her to continue her school correspondence from Spinster's, deliver the baby, and give it up for adoption without anyone having to know any better. But everyone knew.

And me? I'm sentenced to one month.

I feel sorry for her at times. I mean she takes these troubled kids in, and she never asks a dime. But maybe it's that she needs to feel less lonely. I mean, maybe she needs us more than we need her.

My father decided that I should stay with her when he caught Marco and me in the back of his van last Friday night. We weren't naked when he caught us, but if he had come a few minutes later, we would have been. Marco was real cool when my dad slid the van door open. He just said, "Mr. Sharma?" Well, it was kind of stupid actually. What was he expecting my dad to say? "Yes?"

There were no words after that, and there haven't been ever since. Marco got out of the van with his shirt and shoes in his hands. I held my sweater up over myself, hoping that my dad wouldn't notice the bra hanging off the passenger seat, and dad closed the van door behind us and drove the Escort until he could buy another. "There is no fire in hell that would permit me to re-enter that vehicle of Satan." He pronounced it *Shay-thon*. The way the Indians say it is far more evil.

It's strange, but all that I remember of that night was the sound of Marco's motorbike. It took him about six or seven tries before it finally started. I was watching him from my bedroom window and praying he wouldn't flood it. I pulled the curtain back when the engine finally caught. He revved it hard, three times. I thought he was secretly sending me three words: I Love You. But he never looked up. He just buttoned his shirt and drove away.

My dad dropped me off at Spinster's two days after that.

"Do whatever it takes, Ms. Sohi." He turned and drove away, leaving his problem behind. It's funny how he and Marco had that in common.

Spinster's bathroom is my favourite place. It's the only place that has a door that closes. The wallpaper in the bathroom is a galaxy of stars: small and big white specks in a dark blue night sky. No planets – just stars. I can't imagine Spinster picking this wallpaper. I'm sure it was the previous owner's, or else it had to be on sale. Spinster is the repeated small flower print or pinstripe type—definitely not the galaxy type.

When there was a lock, I'd light a candle, turn off the lights and try to find constellations in the reflection of the wallpaper in the mirror. It was so much harder to spot them in reverse. The big dipper was a giant slide with a cardboard box at the bottom. And the little dipper was a broken gear shift.

I learn to spot other things in the stars. I memorize them. My bathroom ritual – a wilted flower, a witch's hat, a penis head, Spinster's door key, a three-legged donkey, a metal ice-cream scoop, and Marco's smile. Marco's smile isn't really a specific constellation that I can spot instantly, forwards and backwards like the others, it's sort of everywhere – kind of in all the constellations, if you look long enough.

Spinster keeps a thick blue butterfly-shaped candle on the counter by the towels. The towels, the sink, and the toilets are red. And so are the seashell-shaped soaps in the navy blue soap tray. It's psychedelic: red, blue and stars for miles. But it was better when there was a lock. At least then I could stand on the toilet seat and blow my smoke out the window, peacefully, without having to jump down and put my cigarette out in the toilet bowl every time I heard a sound.

Today is Sunday, so Spinster is wearing all white except for the Mickey Mouse head on her sweatshirt. Somehow I never pictured Spinster with the mouse. But she always wears stuff like this. I think it makes her feel 'with it'—so that, we, the troubled girls can relate. I have to give her credit though, all the other older Indian women wear long shapeless dresses, in coloured prints of paisley, flowers, or abstract shape patterns that go all the way to the ankles. At least I've seen Spinster's knees.

"Why do you always wear white?" I pour milk into my Cheerios without looking up at her.

"Because it is Sunday," Spinster says.

She walks through to the living room and I smell her *udd* scent follow her – Jasmine.

"Yeah, but why?" I persist from the kitchen.

I stop chewing so that I can hear the sounds from the living room. I wasn't expecting an answer. But maybe a 'cchhup' or an 'oh-foh'. Nothing. Spinster jingles her keys and folds her newspaper to put it away. She pauses while folding, and I guess it's either because she's spotted an interesting headline, or because she's having troubles with her knees. She always gets up on one knee, pauses, and then shifts her weight a bit before the other knee thrusts her up.

"Are you okay?" I say. I can't believe how strange the words sound as they come out of my mouth. I picture Spinster shocked as well—maybe even losing her balance. I cough, hoping it goes unheard. But it doesn't.

"*Chhup!*" She snaps.

Spinster shuffles around in the living room for awhile until finally she jingles her keys again and closes the door. I hear the key turn the outside lock behind her. A familiar sound. Aside from the windows in the attic, the tiny bathroom window that serves as a vent, and the small window above the front door, all the others are barred. Not the thick black prison or penitentiary bars. Too expensive. These ones are the thin red durable plastic kind. It almost looks like the stuff that wraps the fancy apple-pears in Safeway. Only it's plastic and red. I heard it was donated by Bina's family. And I believe it. It had to have come in other colors like black, white, invisible or burgundy or something, but Spinster just had to make a statement with red.

Alone at last. She rarely leaves me alone. I continue my search for the remote and phones. They must be in a real simple place instead of all the complicated tricky spots I've been trying. It would be just like her to put the remote right back in the coffee table's secret sliding drawer, where it's always been. I run for the table, smiling to myself, triumphantly. I open the drawer. Nothing but three 'Get Well Soon' and three 'With Heartfelt Condolences' cards. I guess she must need to use a lot of those as her friends keep dying off. It is sad. But she's old. I picture Spinster first sending the Get Well one and then waiting until she has to write the next. It's like she knows they're going to die, it's just how long they can hang on between the cards.

Spinster takes care of herself. She's only sixty-three. I say only because all of her friends are seventy up, and look ninety-ish. She hardly has them over when she's got one of us hard-to-manage cases staying with her, but once in a while they'll stop for *masala chai, katak batak,* and gossip. I think they come by to get the news on us. There's not much to do when you look ninety and feel dead. Mostly, they get dropped off by one of their daughter-in-laws or sons and picked up exactly half an hour later. They look up to Spinster. She is an angel taking care of Satan's children.

When Sheena's grandma came to visit, I wished I had a grandma. She was old like the others but she didn't avoid me like they did. Once, she sat on the sofa beside me. I didn't put the crossword down. I was doing to her what I thought she was going to do to me. But she didn't pretend I wasn't there. She put her old hand on mine and gently lowered the paper. She read the one and only clue that I had filled in – 'MIZAR'. Nine across, five letters, 'double star'. She could read English!

"Mizar," she said slowly. Her eyes closed – trying to remember. She said it over the over again... like it was important that she remembered. She opened her eyes suddenly and said, "Like in the Big Dipper, right?" I nodded, stunned.

She continued, "The bend in the handle. It can only be seen with a microscope, right? A star that is looking like a star but is two very, very, very close stars, like me and Sapna." She looked at Spinster. "Two very close stars. Sapna and Sathi," she said to me. "Dream and Companion." It was the first time that I had heard Spinster's name. Sapna.

Sathi was so different from the others. How would she know "mizar"? I didn't even ask. I didn't even correct her with 'telescope' when she said microscope. I would have jumped at the chance if it had been anyone else.

I waited for Sathi to come again, but Spinster said, "Who, Sathi? Sathi only comes at the end of the month, every month. Like a landlord." There was something odd about the way she said that. I wanted to ask her more, but you can only ask Spinster general questions. When the questions get specific, Spinster gets vague. So I waited for the end of June. Somehow, it made my sentence at Spinster's seem shorter. I secretly hoped Sathi would answer some questions.

I close the secret drawer in the coffee table. I pull the T.V. out to look at the back. There must be a way to unlock the remote function and turn the set on without it. If I could just watch a few shows a day, I'd get by. I sound like Shiraz uncle. "Just a few gins a day …"

I push the set back and rub the carpet with my sock to get rid of the tracks of evidence. I decide to just keep trying the crosswords in my room until I can get over ten clues. Maybe even get so good that I can try for the American or British papers.

I walk up the stairs and end up standing in the hall staring at Spinster's room door. I can't help my curiosity and the energy that races inside me. I run downstairs and look for tools. I find a paperclip and a bobby pin in the bathroom, a hanger in my closet, and a Bic pen refill by the writing table, where the phone would be if Spinster was home. I climb the stairs and set my tools at her door. I look them over and decide to save the hanger for last and try the paperclip. I hold the door knob with one hand and move the clip around the insides feeling for "the spot". I can normally do it in seconds. I learned it when I had to share the bathroom with my sister. It was the only way. But, Spinster's door is different. There is no magic spot. So, I push and twist randomly, until finally I turn the knob. It was open. She left it open. Gotta be a trap, I think to myself. I close the door quickly and shove the tools under my bed.

I lie on my bed and stare at the ceiling. My stomach feels tight and I can hear my heart thumping loudly in my head. I try to imagine what is behind the door. I try to fill in the gaps of the little bits I know from when she stands in the door frame and I catch bits behind her. I remember the post of the bed. Carved wood. The silk robe, which I think has butterflies or dragons, and the postcard on the dresser mirror. Always there. Stuck in between the frame and the glass, halfway up. Green ink.

It is not more than three minutes before I am standing across her dresser bending the postcard back to see the picture. The Taj Mahal in night lights. Blurry lights in the water, a reflection. The writing is in Hindi. But I recognize one thing at the bottom. '143'—the numbers for I love you. 'I' is one letter, 'love' is four, and 'you' is three: 143. Not spoken, just written. It's an Indian thing. I don't know why they just don't write 'I love you'. I mean, everyone knows what the numbers mean anyway. But like most Indian things, it goes unexplained.

I let go of the postcard and it falls. It leaves behind a clean square of mirror, and a large smudge mark. I panic. I try to fit the postcard back in its square and cover the smudge mark in one move, but this is not possible. "Fuck!" Just saying this word in her home makes me all the more nervous. I picture a tape recorder under her bed, or a sound system in the house that she turns on like an alarm when she leaves. Maybe that's why she spends so much time in her room. Maybe she is screening unusual sounds on the tapes. I think back to the many other times I have tried to turn her door knob. I wonder if the tape recorder would pick up such a small noise. Did she know about all the times I tried to open it? I look under the bed and on the walls for a black box with a red light. I try to listen for the sound of a tape softly humming. Nothing.

I look at the smudge mark on the mirror and then at my reflection. I look just like the *Jaipur* mask in Spinster's living room. With my sleeve I wipe the dust from the rest of the mirror and pull out the postcard to check for any left-over dust. Perfect. I slide the card back in and run to my room. I close her door on my crime in one move.

I pace in my room, just waiting to get startled by her car or a knock at the door. I am almost calm until I remember the stuff on the dresser. It will give me away for sure. I pick up a t-shirt from the floor and go back into her room. Dust. Dust. And more dust. The stuff on the dresser makes the mirror look too clean. One by one, I pick up the lipsticks, an empty perfume bottle, some full ones, creams, a jar of Vaseline, some old imperial shillings, jewellery, a dried flower, a wire brush, a hair net and hairpins, a dish of sweet smelling *suva dhana*, and her reading glasses. I wipe them down and place them in the exact spot I find them. I take one last look around the room, and close it behind me. She won't know.

I must have fallen asleep on my bed, because when I wake up, I can hear Spinster making dinner in the kitchen. If she knew she would have woken me. I walk down the stairs and head straight for the living room.

"If you think I'm going to serve it to you there, you are as mad as a hat," Spinster says.

"I'm coming," I yell back at her.

She doesn't know. I make my way to the table and watch her as much as I can without her suspecting. She sets a plate down in front of me. Lentil *Daal*. My dad would lend me his new car if he saw me eating this shit. I can't complain, really. She pays for the food.

"What about you?" I ask as she puts the lid on the pot and turns the stove to minimum.

"*Urray!* How many questions? You just eat all of it." She points at my plate. "And just remember, I don't serve Oreos at midnight like your parents, you know."

She starts to head upstairs. I panic.

"Where are you going?" Stupid question. There are only three rooms upstairs and a hallway. I try to save myself with: "You're not going to eat with me?"

Spinster climbs back down the stairs and cranes her neck to peer at me. "*Urray, Vah!* I am just going to change my clothes. But only if it is okay with *Memsahib.*" Spinster eyes me closely.

Great. Now, I've gone and made her really suspicious. I was hoping she would go in her room when it was dark. Then she wouldn't notice. And by morning, with any luck and a lot of bedside prayers, a thin film of dust would mask everything. No such luck. Spinster starts up the stairs again.

I eat fast I am so nervous. I try to imagine the possibilities. She might yell at me to come upstairs, she might just call my dad from her room, she might throw things, she might give me a lecture about privacy, she might go through my room – no. None of these are Spinster's thing. As the minutes tick by, I begin to realize that I am right. The minutes turn to hours. Spinster doesn't come down. When I walk slowly upstairs and see that her room light is still on, I know. She knows.

At ten forty in the morning I wake up to the dog across the street barking at the mailman. I check to see if Spinster is home. Her bedroom door is wide open. But as I look closer, I notice there is no door. Just hinges. Hinges and a note: 'I loved him, but he loved Sathi. I keep the postcard. It's all I have left.'

Make Your Own Chai, Mama's Boy!

"You know, I'm not going to just wait around for your boobs to head south." Hafiz spoons the last of the swollen cheerio's into his mouth, and slurps the milk in his bowl.

"I'm throwing in a load of colours, do you want to add anything?"

"I'm serious, Zam." Hafiz is pulling up the sofa cushions, looking for the remote control.

"It's on the TV," Zam goes into the bedroom and sorts through the clothes on the floor.

"What is?" Hafiz yells after her.

Zam raises her voice over the sound of the washer, "THE REMOTE," and picks up a pair of his jeans and an old, pilling, navy Gap sweater. She draws the sweater to her nose and smells the only thing left of him she used to love. That silly, cheap cologne his father gave him for *Eid*. Big Steel. What a name. But it was good. She breathes him in again. "They might as well have called it homos humungous, or machos erectus." She throws the sweater in.

At least they weren't married long, Zamiyah thought. Trying to divide one and a half years of their worthless memorabilia would be like fighting a child for his Halloween stash.

It wasn't going to be long, now. Zamiyah is not stupid. She must be patient because she knows that it will be his first move that will make all of hers appear necessary. Passive aggressive? No. Zam is the frog waiting for the fly. The only difference being, she's the fly and she wants to be caught. She is Caesar and she knows her Brutus. He's her ticket to fly.

She has already found a small, sweet, studio on the beat of the street. She has always wanted to be "alive on the Drive". Commercial Drive. Vancouver's neo-classical street of some very select cross-cultural beings, inter-mingling their auras, paving the path of their destiny with every step they choose, carefree yet careful creatures of the Creator, not bound by time, money, or any gluttonous excess or political poison. Zam is one of these. She will stuff decorative pillows with her Air Canada ties and scarves. Yes, even her Bauvair, Armani and Gucci. She will look for a job in an old bookshop—or even at Joe's Cafe. She will get paid for just 'be'-ing and will come home with the smell of incense and old paper on her clothes and in her hair. She will not call it the "Drive", though. She will remind herself to be cool. Cool on Commercial means wearing your soul with pride. Even the vagabonds are cool. They are so not East side.

Zamiyah surveys the living area, minus Hafiz, of course. Let's see, she thinks, he can have the sofa, the TV, the table lamp, "The Clapper", and even the hookah I got from Turkey. (He loves it. It's his ice breaker. Conversation piece. Things to get things rolling when people come over. He always has his stories ready. All they have to say is, "Wow, what's that?" or "Great hookah pipe!" or "Can you turn that into a bong?" He is ready for them all. He can keep it. He needs it. *I need nothing*, she thinks. Her mantra for 2003.

"What are you just standing there for?" Hafiz's shoed feet are up on the couch, and the rocking wicker (the only other chair in the room aside from the dining chairs in the kitchen) has a stack of newspapers and his Maxim and Penthouse magazines. This is quite blatantly not an invitation to sit down and watch TV together. "Well?" He takes his eyes away from the set and looks at Zamiyah. "Can't you just be normal sometimes?"

"Sure." She knows he hates these one syllable steel walls.

Zamiyah goes back to subtly scan the room and take into account their co-existent stock. "Shit." She thinks to herself. "Music. The fucking CD's." She knows he will fuss. He will count them and divide them in half. Looking towards the rack she quickly scans a few that she can later remove without him even missing them. Kate Bush, Sara, Norah Jones, K.D. Lang, Sinead O'Connor, and Alannis—no—he will fight for her. He only likes the one song because she says *"will she go down on you in a theatre?"* Shallow shit. He was not always this way.

Yes. And Sara. He will make a stink over Sara just because he is that way. He will break her well-kept collection. This she knows. But she will have Suzanne Vega, Peter Gabriel, Simon and Garfunkel, Randy Travis, Anything but the Girl, R.E.M., No Doubt, Harry Chapin, Avril Lavigne, Cher, and Kenny Rogers, Greatest Hits."

"I'm going to have a drink with Hux and Shannon. Do you want to have dinner with Mom?" Hafiz's eyes are on the screen. It's a commercial for Always with wings. His eyes are glazed and dazed and seem to look beyond the computerized simulation of a sanitary napkin growing wings. "She's probably not doing anything."

She thinks of another evening with his mother. On and on and on. Customs, traditions, culture, "in my day we used to".... No. This will stop. And why not today. Say it.

"No."

"What do you mean, "no"? What are you going to be doing?"

The words line up beautifully in her mind and she hears how perfectly they sound even before they fall out of her mouth.

"Tonight?" She says firmly and walks towards the bedroom. "Tonight, I will be *doing nothing.*"

There is only the faint sound of the muted TV behind the bedroom's closed door. A few minutes pass and he hasn't said a thing—which is good, because she isn't waiting for him to. Zamiyah opens her side of the closet and takes down the batik print of an Indian woman bending the branch of a tree to support herself while she removes a thorn from the bottom of her bleeding foot. Just below her foot, beads of blood make trails down the blades of grass. It is funny, because Hafiz's mother gave it to him. It stayed rolled in a cardboard tube for at least a year before she came across it. Hafiz gave it to her willingly but asked her not to put it on display. So there it hung behind her clothes until today. This is the first thing she is taking to the studio today. She has had the keys for over a month now, and still it is bare. This will be the piece that her whole suite will revolve around. She has already matched colors from the woman's sari and the colors of the leaves and the sky to the fabric that she will sew on the throw cushions she will place on the floor. She has no chairs, she has no tables, she doesn't even have a bed. But she has a home.

Little by little she will move in her pieces that make up the picture of the life in her mind. It is sad to have to be dead for so long, she thinks to herself. Living in death is worse than death itself. Zamiyah pushes Hafiz's clothes on his side and lies down and tries to think of only nothing.

"Hafiz, you are a lonely fisherman waiting for a mermaid to bite." It just doesn't happen that way. She gets up and starts folding. "And I am the mermaid ...suffocating." She smiles at her muse's folly. "Only fools think and think and think like this. That is why they never get things done," she thinks again, all the while trying not to think about thinking it. "Because they are always thinking." And this is when it happened, Zamiyah fell into this slouch on the bed and burst out laughing. Hysterically, but with real passion you know, and what's his face will say I wasn't there but I saw it all. I had just come over and he told me she was in the bedroom. When I opened the door, I found her sitting cross-legged on a pile of clothes and holding her gut because she was laughing so hard. He made a big deal when she couldn't tell him why she peed her pants on the laundry. I mean she peed herself laughing, and this part with all due respect to you Zam, this part only you know. Why? What can I say but what I saw. And sure as rain I'll tell you I saw an Indian woman peeing all over submission. She just laughed herself free from those handcuffs and went for it. You know, you can't do things half ways. I tell you, after that pee festival, Zam was suddenly in the mood for some tangos with tension if you know what I mean. Sometimes, when I was "invited to come over" or should I say "temporarily validated for the evening", Zam would always be on the verge. Anything could set her off and she'd just start telling him where to shove it. It was amusingly embarrassing. Every now and then what's his face would look over at me to see if I was grinning or if I seemed at all to be enjoying their fatal showdown, but I always feigned disinterest. I mean the longer it went the better my chances. And that's why I miss her so much. Zam was for real. And I haven't seen that in a long time. But Zam knows her path... she chooses to take scenic detours.

Last Friday Zam cooked up some roast beef with rosemary and garlic with some scalloped potatoes and brown sugared carrots (my favourite, for some reason) and we all knew we were in trouble. Hafiz wasn't too happy I was coming but I think he'd rather that than his mother. What would compel her to invite her Mother-in-law I guess I'll never know now, but as I said, Zam knew her path, she was never one to dine and dazzle and flake out half way through.

The roast was in the oven at 1:30 p.m. I watched her patting and smacking it with spices and herb, and we laughed fiendishly while she pulled out a bag of marijuana and sprinkled the crumbs on the meat.

"Your not serious," I said. Kind of waiting for her to wash it off and start again, but Zam had already scooped up the last of the creamed butter and slapped it on the roast. She started rubbing the weed into the roast until it became a fine powder and resembled the rosemary. I know, I know. You're thinking won't it smell? But Zam had her bases covered, and I wasn't about to challenge the wits of her. She added the other ingredients to a bowl of foil that she made, placed the roast in the center, and gently rolled the foil to seal everything in. Not ten seconds after she put the roast in did she twirl around and light the patchouli incense in the living room. She lit another four throughout the house and explained to me before I even had the chance to ask, "Patchouli masks pot, and that was some grade A shit. Everything's going to be *just fine.*" I loved it when she used to say that because it always was.

I didn't plan on falling in love with Zam. It just happened that way.

So get this now, the roast's smelling up the house, everybody's hungry, and we're all getting ready for what would probably be the last supper – Hafiz's mom actually gets up and says, "Well, I guess I should go to the bathroom and wash my hands, you guys do have a lot of dust, you know." And thank God the phone rang because Zam did not look like she was going to make it through the meal. But she was up to her own thing, and in my experience with her I've noticed the one thing she would enjoy most about people that try to help her is if they wouldn't.

"I'll just pick it up, shall I?" Hafiz's mom was not more than a foot from the phone, there was no interception possibilities.

"Oh no, thank you." She said while Hafiz and Zam looked on in horror. "I appreciate that though. We certainly don't get that kind of service in my area.... What's that?... Oh, no thank you... well now let me see here, does it cost extra? No? Well now that is a good deal ... Well, let's see here, I am always forgetting that stupid area code... Three extra numbers and everything goes in a haywire, right? Yes, 604, 538, 91—"

Hafiz motioned for Zam to get the phone, but she didn't. She let those last two digits through. Just think, she probably thought to herself, now the mother and son can have the same crack dealer." Zam hated his addiction, but she hated what he had become even more. I know there was a time when she really loved him because that was the time she wouldn't love me. So, I guess it's alright that she left and all.

You'd get tired I'm sure—everyone pulling on you this way and that. I like to believe that I will see her again.

"Yes, and I thank you very much. I know that Safeway charges, and getting older is hard I must say. This would be very helpful indeed. Selfish kids I have...none of them told me about this----What's that? Blow? Blow what. Oh mushrooms... mushrooms----chocolate covered—oh no, just plain for salad. I even put them in with curry, sometimes I use those big and black shitcake ones—"

"Mom!" Hafiz reached for the phone but she was the tyrant and there was no stopping what just started. I had to laugh. Zam just opened the oven and checked on the roast like nothing was going on, like it was no big thing that this dealer couldn't figure out who he was talking to.

"Drugs? Oh no. Those I get delivered from Shopper's. They are very good about that. Anyway, if you don't mind—what was your name—Oh Kite... Kite like flying kite?... now that's interesting. Well Kite, we are just having dinner right now, would you call back if you need anything... yes....yes that's right... Oh no, I don't stay here, I'm his mother."

Dial tone.

The evening was a blast. Zam put her love into our stomachs and we all laughed thinking all the while that it was the wine. Casielliero de Diablo. No kidding. That was the name. All I had to hear was Diablo and I knew no other wine would dare to share its name. The roast was marinated over night in the stuff. I tell you that hunk of meat was liquored and basted with pot and roasted on low for hours. The scalloped potatoes came out a bit crispy where some of the cheese had burned, but Zam just turned them into stuffed spuds with sour cream and simulated bacon bits which by the way, Hafiz's mom refused to eat. Hafiz didn't say much but I think he knew something was up. He never forgave her for me and she could never forgive him for making her want more. He was one of those designer limited edition husbands that stayed in the showroom and was not to be tested on the road. He knows this, I'm sure.

While Hafiz was at work on Wednesday, Zam packed and shipped all of her things by cab to her new studio. She had a lot more than she had bargained for so she ended up having to take like six trips. She knew I could have easily taken the day off and helped her with my Honda, I mean it's a hatchback and all and could probably haul more per trip and save some money, but everything is not about that. Zam wanted to be free of anything that stopped her from moving on. She used her saved up money for their trip to fucking Honolulu. Can you believe that? That's where he was taking her. And I remember Hafiz saying that it was the international meeting place of beautiful bodies. Gay, eh? I mean dumb and gay. I would have taken her to South America, London, England, or Greece. Yeah Hafiz had a body. To heteros he was a babe. And Zam was an Indian princess with a fire in her eyes. Their wedding picture is adorable. That photographer managed to click at just the right moment. They are both looking at each other and for that moment and probably that moment alone they were on the same page. But this marriage was a deal for Hafiz. It meant a better lifestyle... and more importantly, it meant money. Hafiz's mom deserves what's coming to her that's all I can say. She will just lose her mind when she finds out that her son has been abandoned—oh what shame she will have to endure. Yeah right. She shouldn't have promised him 10, 000.00 dollars in advance if they got married three months earlier. Maybe they might have known. But, I guess these days even love can be bought. Not a hell of a lot for such a pretty mistake.

Zam never did call and I don't suspect she will. She has made her move and I know roughly where she is should I just need to look at her. You know, make sure she's safe and hanging with a healthy group. Oh look at me... I'm just another Hafiz. Just another Mother-in-Law. Just another shackle. I know how to step gracefully out of a dance and offer my partner to another.

People cut in all the time... I just wanted to know which song was our last. At least he shared the note with me:

Dear Hafiz, Mom and Shay,

I don't know when you'll come across this, but I haven't made it too hard to find. I am happy and well and the only thing I wish to ask of you is to just let me stay this way. Please don't try to find me... this will just make things painful and complicated. Anything of mine can be left in the storage shed. I still have my key. Seasons change and sometimes you just think you're never going to make it out of the winter. And then suddenly you spot it... a tulip, soaring for the sun.

Zamiyhah

This is a Good Thing

Mealtimes I think of her. For dessert I always pick vanilla. That's what she would have picked if she were here with me. Asha said chocolate made her teeth sting and was too sweet, and butterscotch was too much like the stuff on Halloween apples. Vanilla was a simple pleasure. Simple and pure.

I called her Asha and she called me Amin. A and A. We were meant to be. Written by the gods. I try not to think about her now. But I write about her all the time. No one but Godley understands my stuff, so he is the only one I share it with.

Asha is the first one I ever wrote about. She got inside me, you know? I vowed to never fall in love on account that I like to fuck so much. Different flavours, different savours. Well, I'm up front about it. I say this right away – even before anything happens. I usually say something like, "I'm just trying you out. You know. Test driving you." Most of them don't object. They never object. They want to be driven. They don't have to say anything. I just know. I guess you could say I'm kind of blessed that way. Well, not so much in the size department. I'm 3" at best. Mother said it was a good size. She said that it could get painful and cause sexual diseases if it was too big.

But Asha, well now she got to me – and that's why I had to let her go. All of a sudden I wasn't doing the driving. I was being driven. I loved her. Especially in the mornings before she left. At night she would look tired and her eyes would become heavy. So we did it in the mornings. We were a secret. A morning secret. By the time the sun set, Asha set. She was tired and worn down from classes all day. Those bastards at school expected too much from her. But she never complained. She was going to make it some day. This she told me. She wanted to be a famous photographer. She took pictures all the time, and I saw some of them. They were really quite good. She took this picture once of a candle burning on an oak table in the living room. The wax from the candle had formed a puddle on the wood in the shape of a heart. And the glow around the flame was a perfect halo. It was really quite something... a heart. Imagine that. Hot wax on wood. She taught me things. She was so quiet and dainty. I watched her once put on her nightgown in front of her window, in the soft pale light of the moon. As she stood there I could see her slim figure outlined. It was the sliver of space between her thighs that made me want her again and again – that sliver of light between the shadow of her thighs.

Asha, Asha,
Smooth as soap.
Asha, Asha,
Could not cope.
Asha was the best.
A cut above the rest.

My first poem. I know. It sucks. Well, I wasn't as good as I am now that she's gone. I wrote this one on the second Sunday. Asha let me taste her. Stiff and unyielding, but eventually she gave in to my wiles. They all do. Sweet and warm like rice pudding. She didn't smell like some of the older women I have been with in the past. No heavy perfumes between their legs trying so desperately to hide the truth. She was clean and new and she always smelled like baby powder. Before and after showers. Soft and sweet and always obliging. Always quiet like some great philosopher with something very important on her mind. But whatever she might have been thinking, she never shared it with me. And maybe I liked it that way. To be honest. The more they talk, the easier it is to discover how different you really are. This way there was nothing to fight about. No fights over dinner, no fights in the park, no fights about where to go or not go. No fights, just a safe secret. And a lot of fucking.

And the best part about Asha was that she was always wet. Always wet for me. In the beginning it hurt a little. My skin would cut and rip. I would have to bandage it with cold cream and wait for it to heal. Asha said that it would burn when she peed. But after the second Sunday we were in sync.

Asha on the periphery,
While I am looking in.

Godley was the real poet before he came here. He even got paid for a few. He had words up his sleeves, and all kinds of words. I told him I used to paint houses for House Jackets on Main and Columbia. He said he knew the place. "Dead end," he said. "As soon as we get back to reality I'll set you up with my people, and if you work hard, you might just get one published." He's my private tutor, if you will. He gives me assignments. Three words a day on the toilet—Godley's got the mini Webster's Dictionary sitting on the back of the john. He says I have to learn three new words a day and define them, as well as two full sentences correctly using the words. Every day I place my assignment in Godley's cigar box for marking. Three a day means about a whole dictionary's worth of words by the end. He says my vocabulary could sure use some expanding. My very own dictionary.

"A lot of crap gets published just on account that people don't know what the poet's even talking about." He says, "Stay vague and use big words. People love that shit."

Asha is on the periphery.
While I am looking in.
The verisimilitude of Asha everywhere
She is a watercolour painting in the rain.
A hallucination made of sand.
A mirage of swirly colors,
All melting into inebriated beads.

Godley says this one's got rhythm and movement and potential. He says the only problem is my name. Amin. He says no one's going to buy that. So I look up other words: Agate, Aim, Ague, Abet, Abel. Abrade.

"Abrade's good." He says. "I think it even means something cool. Yeah, it's a keeper." Godley's real name was Geoffrey.

Yesterday, they took us out before breakfast at around five in the morning. Some kind of exercise. I woke up kind of groggy, but Godley was cursing something awful. New words I hadn't ever heard before. The sky was "Cobalt Blue" and the clouds were "Eggshell White". I told Godley these were some of the names of the paints we used to mix at the shop. He just kept on cursing. You just add two or three drops of another colour base and everything changes. You can invent new colours all day. Just swirl it in before mixing. That way if you don't like your creation you can scoop most of the base and start all over again. I'm better at my colours than my words, Godley says.

But House jackets might have a copyright on colours like Crayola. I'll have to check.

We had to walk in single file towards the Eatery. There were about twenty of us in each group. Godley was about ten behind me and Cunningham was in front. Well, Cunningham kept nodding off while he was walking. Stumbling and then catching himself right before he'd fall. I could tell from behind. As soon as his head would start to look like it was getting kind of heavy, I'd nudge him forward. By the fourth or fifth time he was getting a little pissed off, as if I was responsible for this morning's promenade. (That's just another word for walk in French or Spanish, I can't remember). So, anyway all of a sudden he just turned right around and socked me one and called me an ignorant dumb fuck of a paki. Well, I fell and the whole line behind me fell like dominoes. And where the fall began was where the blame was cast. Cunningham was just standing there and grinning at me, while massaging his right hand. That's when the suit glared at me, and said, "What time did you get to bed 513?" Like I'm in the Army or something. The other guards they call you by name, but this one, well she was a woman. And women have been out to get me ever since the day I was born. I could tell by the way she looked at my crotch. So I said, "Same time as you, don't you remember?" Cunningham stopped smiling and I could hear Godley just cracking up along with some of the others behind me. This one short encounter got me fifty push ups and no desserts for a week.

Godley said I should have just fucked her right there. She was alone. The other guys would have all unzipped, too. He said it was dark and we could have all kept walking like we were being led and just passed her down the line. None of the other groups would have even noticed. Godley said he could have muted her with his sleeve and de-gunned her in less than thirty seconds. And I believe him. I've seen him eat big wads and wads of paper. Poems he doesn't want anyone to find.

But she was wretched and old. Damaged goods. Not my type for sure. She might have been worth the fuck when she was young—when she carried a colourful lunch box with her favourite cartoon or super-hero instead of a paper bag to school. Maybe when she would sit in front of the television watching "I Dream of Jeanie", with her legs spread, and her dress rising up past her thighs, eyes glued, body tight, cute pig-tails in ribbons. But not now with her "Nice and not so Easy" blonde-dyed hair hanging out from the back of her cap in a dry frizzy pony tail and her artificially tanned face glowing in a thin coat of Nivea. Even at five in the morning she managed to find the time to blot her wrinkled lips in Candy Apple Red.

Asha pour more.
Pour more for Abrade.
I'll sip your serum until you make more,
For me to sip again.
Fresh cream on Sunday morning
Secret
Now you will stay young
I have preserved you with my love
Embalmed you in a sweet syrup of a memory
I dream you into my hand
My hand is your blossom gripping me
So tight and clean
I dream you in my hand

Asha on the swings with her hair blowing free. She never tied it. I asked her to set it free. Long black strands fell in soft curls around her small heart-shaped brown face. Breathtaking. I never had to lay down the law. I just asked and it would be so. The next day she gave me all her silk headbands and collared barrettes and made me promise I would always love her. I did.

After school on Fridays Asha would sit on the swings and yell, "Higher! Higher!" I would run behind her and push her as high as I could and then spin around and do it again. I never fucked her in the park. Even she felt uncomfortable with that and I respected her. But sometimes I would sit her on top of me on the swing and pump us into the air. Just feeling her rub against me—even through our clothes—was enough to make me cum. And I would show Asha and she would get this confused look on her face and scrunch her eyebrows and say, "This is a good thing?" And I would assure her, "Yes, Asha this is a very good thing. This is a symbol of my love for you."

Monday through Thursday Asha's mother would take her to Jazz class. My sister was adamant that her daughter should become a professional dancer and neglected Asha's love for photography. Asha would begrudgingly go and not get home until six thirty in the evening. But Fridays was the day they entrusted me to pick her up from school and we would spend some quality time together in the park. The last Friday we were together I even confessed to her that she was the only one I would ever love. I told her I would be faithful and she even understood the word.

Asha bleeding in the sand
Hold my hand
Coagulated beads of
Sacrificial red pearls
Bleed for me

Godley says they're getting kind of dreary. Melancholic. I had to look that up. It sounded like some kind a disease. He finally came out and asked me how she died. I tell him that it's none of his fucking business.

"So that's why you're in here? Because you killed some childhood sweetheart?"

"No." I say. "Why are you in here?"

"Coca Cola shipment," he says and puts his finger to his nose. "Could have been a handsome sum, and I would have never had to write a poem again—not for money anyway."

We don't talk for a day and a half, which is a lot considering we are all each other has. But he can get that way, moody and all, so mostly I just let him be.

The Suits put us in the cell early and that's when Godley breaks the silence with, "I am not going to be your teacher anymore, I have decided, so you should just go back to House Coats or House Jackets, or whatever the name of that stupid place is. And don't try calling me either, because I'll just change my number." He turns and walks to the corner of the cell. I follow him, but keep my distance just in case.

"But I've done my words, I just haven't handed them in." I try to show him the papers.

"You stay away from me!" Godley turns around and starts yelling loud enough to send the Suits over.

I stand still. As still as if he's aiming a 45 calibre at my heart. But Godley's just pointing his finger. He is inches away from my throat.

"How old was she, you mother fucker?"

"Twenty-nine," I say, watching his hands the whole time. But Godley's eye is twitching and he looks like he is going to mash up my face so I call out for the guards. Godley reaches for his cigar box and throws it at my head and all of my assignments go flying everywhere.

"You fucking liar!" He pins me against the bunk and with one hand he presses my head into the wall and I feel like it's going explode.

"I'm not lying." The words barely come out. I am gasping for air and he releases me when he hears them coming.

"Cut it out, you guys. What seems to be the problem here?" It's Blondie. Two other Suits are standing behind her, equipped with cuffs and heel ties. I know I'm done for by the way she is eyeing me. She's always wanted me.

Godley's shaking and sweating like a madman. "You guys got me bunked up with a fucking child-molester!

One of the guards is looking at me and snickering like he's going to have a go at me next.

"I am not a child— " But before I can finish, Godley takes a leap at me and starts taking shots at my head. One after the other, and I all I can hear is a jingling set of keys and Blondie shouting, "Alright, that's enough, get off of him. I said enough."

But by the time they pull him off of me, his fists are covered in blood and I can feel it drying, sticky on my face. I taste it in my mouth and I remember Asha. I only hit her once. I only hit her once. I only hit her once. I say this over and over until I feel better. My head is throbbing and I feel like I am going to throw up I am so dizzy. It takes both of them to drag Godley away, but I yell after him, "I loved her, you bastard. I'm in here because I killed her, not because I loved her."

The suit asks Blondie if she'll be okay with me while he goes and calls for backup.

"Oh, sure. Me and 513 will be just fine. Seems we need to have a bit of a talk, don't we, 513?" Blondie's just waiting to be alone with me.

"Just make sure you stay on the outside." He says, and then looks at me. "And you just settle down over there. Or I'll be back for you."

"We'll be fine." Blondie waves him off. "Go on already."

I look around me at all the little papers with red markings on the floor. My head is pulsing.

"Settle down, 513. Grab yourself a bunk and just take it easy, now. You really don't want him coming back."

"I loved her," I blurt out.

"Yes." Blondie looks away—jealous, I'm sure. She takes out her notebook and a pen and starts with the questions. "Can you tell me how this all started?"

I wipe my face with my shirt, but most of the blood has dried.

"Use the sink." She says.

I walk over to the sink, and I am sure she is looking at my ass. While I run the hot water, I turn around quickly to try and catch her, but she has already turned her head. I press the towel against my face and it burns something awful.

"It burns. Can you blow on it?" I say.

Blondie just ignores me and looks right into my eyes and asks again. "How did it start, 513?"

I pull my chair right up to the bars. I am not afraid of her.

"Right here," I say, cupping my balls. "Can you blow?"

"You're going to get in some pretty deep shit for this. I suggest you start cooperating." She is pretending not to be enjoying herself, but I know she is. She wanted to be alone with me the whole time, now's her chance. I'll make it worth her efforts.

I rub myself while I am talking. It's almost unnoticeable, but Blondie's looked there twice already. It's probably the closest this old hag's been to a man in a very long time.

"He asked me how old my mother was." I say. And all the while, I am getting more and more excited. She's even starting to look like my mother. When she was dying, one of her last wishes was to be dyed blonde. The dead brunette was dyed blonde---she laid there looking like she was wearing some kind of wig. She forgot to ask that her dead eyebrows be lightened.

"So what you are saying is that you didn't think it was very polite of him to ask your mother's age?" Blondie's a bitch and she plays her part perfectly.

"No. I just didn't think it was any of his business calling me a mother fucker." I say, rubbing myself even harder.

Blondie's writing all of this down, but she's still got time to get a few peeks in.

66

"Well, are you?"

I unzip myself and expose myself to her. "It's as big as it's going to get. Do you like it?" I rub my head and it throbs for her.

"Are you?"

"Yes." I say. "Will you blow it?"

"Did you rape your mother, 513?"

Blondie's sticking to the questions, but I know her pussy is wet for me. I can smell it. She doesn't smell near as bad as mother did.

"She raped me."

"So now you rape young girls and kill them?"

"No." I continue masturbating for her. I know she wants to see me explode for her. "I loved Asha."

"Who's Asha?"

"My niece."

"And you loved her the way your mother loved you?" Blondie's shifting nervously in her seat—a good sign.

> Asha bleeding in the sand
> Hold my hand
> I'll dream you into another place
> Hold my hand

I remember how Asha used to do the same. She'd get all nervous and embarrassed, but I would ease her into the routine. She really got the hang of it. She got so good at it, she wanted to make me cum all the time. Even at the dinner table, Asha would stretch out her leg and rub it against my crotch. When it got hard she would smile like she had done something right. I would tell her I loved our secret and that one day it wouldn't have to be. I promised her I would take her far away from her mom and dad and she could take pictures of different places all over the world. And really I would have. But that's when I realized what she was up to. She had me trapped. She was much smarter than the others. She wanted me all to herself—too smart for her own good. I had to do something, or lose control. And I wasn't going to have that.

Blondie's still taking notes but her writing is not as neat as it was before. I know she likes my stub. It may be short but it's thick and satisfying. It is a good thing. I rub it harder and harder. She doesn't bother me with her questions.

"Could you put your dick away?" Blondie's pen falls. "I am not amused."

"Why don't you come in here and I'm sure I can find a place for it."

Blondie's playing it cool, but I know she's considering it. My dick is pink from the dried blood on my hand. I spit into my hand for more lube and prepare to give her a show.

"Did you kill your mother, too?"

She's got balls. "Fuck you!" Now I've lost my rhythm and mood altogether. I kick the bars and spit at her, purposely missing. "Fuck you and your questions! Some job you have, stuck in here sucking the rest of us of? Is your mom proud of you?"

"It's just you and me, 513. Just you and me." Blondie closes her notebook and stands up. "Did you kill your mother?

"No! I did not!" I stare into my bloody hand. "Just Asha."

Blondie shakes her head and begins to walk away. I hear her boots clicking with authority.

"My mother...My mother, she killed me."

Car Band Copy

I am walking to the *Paanwala*, and this is when I find out. *Didi* (sister), well, this is what I gonna call her for now, is sending me to get some *paan* (betel leaf) for Mahrun *Bhaya, her husband*. Now, this part is not something too different. My Mahrun *Bhaya*, well you see, he need suck *paan* much like you and me need drink water. But it's the way she say it. You see? She say, "Priya, go and get some *paan* for *Bapa.*" *Bapa*. (Dad). Just like that. And when she say it, you see Mahrun *Bhaya*, he be reading the paper like as before. He is not even looking up. And even when I ask, "What?" like if I didn't hear it the first time, she just ask again. Same like before. Only this time louder. *"Jaldi ja paan lijiye, Bapa ke liye."* (Hurry, now and get some *paan* for Dad.) It's this that make me start thinking while I am walking to the *Paanwala*. Sometime people they say things and they not always thinking. But when I start to thinking, then I think it is not so simple they be making the same mistake twice.

Now you must not get me wrong way. I am not trying to play like I am no private detector like on the TV, truly. We do not even have a TV. I am just trying to say the story like it happen. Just like it happen.

So, she call Mahrun *Bhaya*, Dad. Now I know people they gonna make mistake, but it is just the kind of mistake they are making

70

that get me start to thinking. I been cheated by the fruit vendor before. My math is not good like my English. So he take me for ten rupees on a bag of bananas. That is my mistake. See? And I done and get a nice good scolding by *Didi's* husband, who become my brother-of-law Mahrun. But, I am telling you truly, while he be hitting on me with the belt, I never gone and said, "Please stop, *Bapa.*" Right?

So, is on the way to the *Paanwala,* I see this boy. You know, about two times me. He is older and he think he is so smart because he go and walk faster on the side road. Well, he may be richer, but not smarter. He is wearing them rich-like running shoes like the kind they show on TV. We never buy TV stuff because Mahrun say the people who go and buy TV stuff end up living in the TV when they get older. But sometime I get to thinking that that Mahrun he be lying. Because in Central District Nairobi, where little girls are not supposed to go alone, is a TV in the Portman bus station. It is a very small TV and it is chain to the ground like a bicycle, but it is the only TV I am ever seeing with my own eye. You see sometime when my skin be too sore to lie on the floor at night, I go quiet pass the door, and no one seem to know or care at night where I go. So I see on the Portman TV little babies. Yes real live crying babies. I never hear them crying because this TV at the Portman bus station is not having any noise, but I see them with open mouth and shut eyes, and I start to thinking, them babies, well they be too small to buy TV stuff. So, that Mahrun, he lie. But when I tell *Didi,* she start to cry real bad. I think she know about these babies, too.

So, I walk fast than the boy and then the boy he start to walk fast than me. He is white with long yellow string hair, and his legs they be chopping like big scissors. Just then a bicycle pass real quick on his side. Yellow Hair bump into me real hard.

71

"Watch out!" he yell at me.

"You watch out!" I yell back. And we stand there on the side of the road. I am looking at him while he be looking at me. I am not too scared, but when he pushes me on my shoulder I put my hands up straight away.

"Oh, so you want a fight?" He say. But I don't want fight.

"No." I say.

"Good, because you be in real trouble if you want fight." He say, with angry face. But he no scare me.

I walk behind him until we get to Banga Street. There is more people there and the Banga trees are like green walls and so I know if I don't walk fast I gonna lose him. My heart is beating fast and I know I am just ten step away from *Paanwala*. So, I can run in the store and never have to see this stupid Yellow Hair again. By the way he be wearing TV stuff and by the way he is going home I know he going to the rich district, so I tell him before he cross the road.

"You know, I never before seen no boy wanting fight with a girl." I say. I know I am close to crying, but I try hard not to show him I am scare. Because I am more scare of this Yellow Hair than I am of Mahrun. When Mahrun hit me it is easy because I know how it gonna feel.

But just then this Yellow Hair, he start laughing, like as if he seeing something funny in the market. But he be looking straight at me. All the people, they start to looking to see what he find so funny in me. And before I can stop it I am crying right there. Hard like *Didi*. So I start to run. I pass the *Paanwala* and turn into the alley of Ashruda.

72

They call it her alley because she call it hers first. And because no one else gone and say it theirs, it become Ashruda alley.

I am sitting there crying. I cry even more because I know that *Didi* will tell Mahrun, and then it gonna be even bigger trouble. And all because of this stupid Yellow Hair. When I look up at Ashruda's window, I see her looking back at me. She ask me to come and have some warm milk.

I am telling her so many times that I am allergy to milk but Ashruda she getting old. So I tell her nice-like that I must go back or they will worry at home. Ashruda say okay and then straight away she ask me: "How is your mother? You and mom look just like car band copy."

What this car band copy? And then I start thinking again. I am seeing Ashruda three and sometime four time a week, because I am getting Mahrun's *paan,* but Ashruda always say, "How is Roshi *Didi?* (sister) So I ask her today, "Why are you say mom , Ashruda Bai?"

But Ashruda, she play like she not hear me, and put her head in her window fast like a turtle in a shell. So, I call to her.

"Ashruda Bai! Ashruda Bai!" I say loud. And Ashruda, I know she hear me because it is too hot and no one close their window in September in Nairobi. Maybe in Nakuru. But no one close it in Nairobi. Only in the rich district when they keep small boxes that look like little TV's inside the window. And these boxes make a wind like the cool watermelon that we eat on birthdays. I am not ever feeling this wind before, but some things I just know.

So, when I call Ashruda one last time, this same Yellow Hair, he come into Ashruda alley. Now I getting real scare because this Ashruda she not listening to me, and if this boy want to hurt me right here, no one is gonna come and get me safe. So I say to Yellow Hair as he be walking close, and I look him straight in the eye, "You want to have four rupees? You can have it." I try and think of what stories I will tell when I get home. Mahrun will say that I am buying candy for myself, and if I say no he will beat me. And if I say yes, he will surely beat me. So I know I gonna say no. And then *Didi* will tell me not to make so much trouble for her husband. If it not for him, we are sure to starve and die. He is a good man. *Didi* always be saying this. He is a good man. Priya, you know Mahrun is a good man. If I don't want to get hurt I should do and behave like a good girl. *Didi* will tell me all over and over again about when she carried the rice and potato bags for our mother, and how our mother liked to laugh so loud all the villagers called her *Khili Bhai* (Laughing Lady). But this Ashruda *Bai* go and call *Didi, mother?* Why? And *Didi* go and call Mahrun *Bapa*.

Yellow Hair be walking close now, and he take his hand out from his pocket, and so I give him the rupees. I save one in my pocket and I start to praying to all of the gods all at one time that he will not be checking in my clothes for more rupees or something more. When Yellow Hair getting real close I tell him not to touch me. But Yellow Hair he just be giving me back *Didi's* rupees. I put my hand in his and he pull me up like an elephant trunk.

"You're a girl?" He say and he smile real big now.

"Yes!" I am not knowing why he say this so I ask him straight, "Why you say this?"

"Well, you don't look like no girl." He say "I never seen no girl with so short hair."

I tell him that I cut my hair short so when I go out at night nobody be bother no little boy. I tell him the truth. I tell him everything. And

Yellow Hair he is listen to me. He listen to me so long that I start to be telling him about the babies in the TV. I don't know why I be telling him, but this Yellow Hair he be laughing so big.

"That Mahrun guy sound like a good and nothing loser." He say

"I start to saying 'yeah' like Yellow Hair because he be saying it. And when I say it I feel like I can lift him like an elephant.

When we be walking away from Ashruda alley, I look back to the window and see quick moving. I know she is seeing and I know she is hearing. She is play like she not home but I know she be watching.

Yellow Hair say that maybe he can come and talk to my sister. I know he be looking at Mahrun's red hand mark on my arm.

"No." I say fast. "Mahrun will kill you, too. Even if you are Indian he will kill you."

Yellow Hair say nothing after this about talking to Didi, but now I start to thinking about things again. Yellow Hair say, "You should not think so much or you run out your battery." Yellow hair be pointing to his head. Yellow Hair English is good like he be one of the TV people. I laugh with Yellow Hair, but most of the time I am not knowing why.

We walk to Arandi Street, and I am feeling like they all be watching me. Maybe they be looking at my yellow dress. It is so brown now that I be calling it my brown dress, but truly it was yellow one time before. I only been one time to the rich district before with Didi's boss Shaira. Shaira take me when she need me to carry her packages. Shaira buy many things from Arandi Market, so many things that Shaira not know when her feather hair pin go missing.

When I am with Shaira, I am her servant. When I am with Yellow Hair, I am his wife. Yellow hair has no belt and he will buy me a TV, and maybe sometime even some TV stuff. Yellow Hair is walking in long fast step. He does not know I am his wife, so I run beside him. He is old than me but I am tall.

Mahrun always say, "Tall women never gonna get them a husband. Finding a husband gonna be like pulling a seedless date straight off tree." So, when he wake up in the morning, he always be pressing down hard on my head with his hand. "Your mother, she was very tall," he say, "and I am needing do this for help you. You must try and stunt your grow. Stunt your grow. Don't worry I will help you. No man ever gonna marry such tall bride. Man like look down at his woman."

I know Yellow Hair is taking me to his home, but I am not asking, just following. I want to go with Yellow Hair so I am not worried about Mahrun's anger today. *Didi* will be worry, but there is no public phone in the gas station where Mahrun is working so he will not be knowing up to 5:30.

Yellow Hair say he is seventeen, so I am thinking seven year different is not too bad. But I don't ask him what he think. He may be think I am too fast to ask these things. But I am not a fast girl. I am just thinking fast. Yellow Hair is wearing blue jean short. He is looking so special than all the people they be walking past us. When we get to the Nairobi Shopping Plaza I know I am very far from my home. I see *Didi* in my head. *Bapa,* she says. She call Mahrun, Dad.

I feel the rupees in my pocket. I want to buy a thin flower skirt like the kind that are blowing even when there is no wind. Yellow Hair is talking to me but sometime he is looking at the taller girls in the street.

When he do this I start to talking more so he will look at me. You see, Yellow Hair don't matter if the girl is white, black or brown. Yellow Hair, he like looking at girl. But I know he most special like look at me.

"You like look at me?" I say.

Yellow Hair, well, he is not surprise. He say in a more deep voice, "Yeah."

I go and tell Yellow Hair about my *Didi*. I tell him *Didi* mean sister, but he say he know.

"Your sister call Mahrun, 'Dad'?" He make a face. "Why she go and do that?"

I go and tell this Yellow Hair that my dad die before I was born and all I have is my *Didi*.

Yellow Hair say, "I'm sorry." He say this sweet like kiwi.

"It's okay. *Didi* say my mother been dead for a long time, too. I never know my mother. My *Didi* say she die in fire. I too young to know," I say. Yellow Hair he hold my hand strong while we crossing *Habari Auto Shop*. I cannot read the sign, but I know the name because Mahrun he be working here last summer. I look and see Harvinder. He be waving at me and Yellow Hair, and smiling. I know he see me holding Yellow Hair hand, but I don't care. Harvinder fire Mahrun for being a drunker, so Mahrun say he never gonna talk to Harvinder on his dead body. That's what he say.

Yellow Hair still be thinking about my mother because he say, "Do you have a picture of your mom?"

"Only in my head. *Didi* say everything getting burn in the house. She just taking our clothes and some money to come to Nairobi. *Didi*

77

she take shorthand so she can find work. But when we get here this Mahrun marry her straight away. Now, he keep her in the home to take care of him. He is try and try to make her pregnant, but no babies. So he hate me and he hate her and I hate him. He even ask her one day and I am listen with my own ear, he say 'We must get rid of Priya. Find her husband, then all gonna be okay. She be taking too much of time and too much of food.' *Didi* she start screaming straight away and crying and say, 'Not on her dead body', and they sleep."

"Weeeerd." Yellow Hair say funny word.

"Yeah." I say like Yellow Hair say yeah.

"But no pictures?"

"No pictures. But is okay. *Didi,* she say that everyone say she and mom look like car band copy." I think of Ashruda Bai saying this word. This Yellow Hair maybe know what this mean because he not be asking me.

While we walking, one black woman with just one long earring she walking fast as us. When she get close she slow down and point at her hand and ask Yellow Hair for, "Excuse me do you have a time please?"

This black woman tie big green scarf in her hair like a drum and she not be looking at me and she not be looking at my hand holding Yellow Hair. She just be looking straight in Yellow Hair blue eye like she never seen the ocean before.

"Three-twenty." Yellow hair tell this woman.

Then, this woman go and touch Yellow Hair shoulder and be saying, "Thank-you. Thank you. I me place my watch so I little rush.

Thank you." When she walk away I am wanting to pull on this one earring hard like it be making the hole big to fit five or six earring.

"Why she think you some special superman because you have watch? Why she not ask him?" I am pointing to the man who be walking just next us.

But Yellow Hair he say nothing. He just smile and hold my hand a little tight now.

"Do you like to look down on me?" I look up and ask Yellow Hair who still be smiling.

"No." He say, and swing my hand a little.

And that's when I look up at the sky. It is there all the time, but I am looking at it now. As if like it not been there up to now.

Sari Status

Jaya stared into her lap, horrified.

The Sharma sisters whispered to each other without turning their heads or moving their lips – ventriloquists, Indian Barbie dolls. Even at thirty-three, the twins still wore matching outfits waiting for suitors. This day, fuchsia and olive green two-tone raw silk saris with golden embroidered trims. Only the Sharma sisters could pull off such a thing. Both sisters in tightly wound "I'm still a virgin" French braids, laced with baby's breath. The people talked, of course. *Why are they not married, yet?* But in all fairness, they truly were as beautiful as the Bollywood film stars. "Something must be wrong with them," one gossiper started. "They are probably unable to bear sons," another finished. They didn't say children. The Indian community are sophisticated gossipers. To some it is a highly reputable art and even sometimes, a paid profession.

Jaya sat on the decorated bride's chair and wiped vomit from her chin, carefully so as not to smudge her painted lips. Jaya never wore lipstick. The furthest she would dare go was tinted lip balm. Her lips were already the color of kidney beans. A soft, nice, natural color by God, not "Rose Petal Dust" by Maybelleine. Jaya watched the spectators watching her. She was the bride... so she was the show. And brides never throw up the night before the wedding.

It was the night of Jaya's *mandvo* – the giving away ceremony. The bride's family and friends prepare her for her new life with her husband; the husband who would then open her to the sensual wonders and joys of sex. Things she already knew too well with me. But I was the secret Jaya just could not bring herself to share. She feigned ignorance the night her mother told her about the cumbersome pains of intercourse, and how she would eventually get used to it and give into her husband's wishes and blah, blah, blah. Jaya was a lesbian of four years.

Jaya thought about Van Gogh and *chai* lattes while her mother told her about the male's private parts. Once her mother went on and on to her younger brother about the dangers of excessive masturbation with an accent as thick as oatmeal. *"It vill bend and ju vill not be able to pee anymore."* Ahmed was only fourteen and not impressed. But Jaya went into his room that night and slipped "The Joy of Sex" under his pillow. Jaya's mother was happy to see that he was spending more time in his room and not watching so much television. But his grades stayed the same. If not, worse.

The bride's family hosts the *mandvo,* and this one ran a bill of almost six thousand dollars – gold gifts not included. Her family was not a wealthy one, but to be honest, on this day, they were only too happy to see this ache live in someone else's head. Saving for this kind of dowry was like buying good stock. You lose a little money up front, but the payback is always worth the down.

Jaya knew her brother would never have been born had she been a boy. Her parents had originally only wanted one child. And she was nothing shy of a blatant mistake. Her mother had even told her of the special herbs and potions the local city Shaman had given her in order that she might produce a boy. Counting and marking the

81

days on the calendar, her mother watched the moon – and even blamed the moon in the end. *"Ju know, I really to this day think it was not pull enough,"* she told Jaya. Were they still in India Jaya knew she might have easily been just buried in the backyard like thousands of other baby girls. She pictured the small freshly dug graves that were never objected to by onlookers; onlookers who undoubtedly empathized with the ill-fortune of the family, and most likely even aided in the doing away of the still crying, still kicking infant.

Jaya had watched one such burial in a documentary on Calcutta girls on TV. To this day she has nightmares. The details never change. Just the faces.

Her eyes, her best feature, were faded this day. Her sister-in-law from London had worked on them for one solid hour. Normally, almond-shaped with tiny flecks of dark chocolate, today they were just heavily shadowed, and bewildered. Dark circles had developed soon after the announcement of this marriage.

Jaya's mother rushed to her daughter's aid, like the infamous mother characters in Indian films. Mature heavy-chested heroines of the fifties and sixties were now being reduced to mother roles. They are always over-acting in a desperate attempt to outshine the new and improved slender heroines of tomorrow. Jaya looked at her mother, who looked back and forth from Jaya to the onlookers, half-sympathetic, half-humiliated at the scene.

Jaya attempted some kind of reasoning with her mother, "Mom, I just really don't think I can go through with all of this. I just don't think–"

"Quiet now, Jaya! I mean really. Vhat kind of a time is it for ju to be thinking. Stop all this garbage talk and vipe that look off jore face. Just smile. Come on, smile. They are all looking, now." She knelt down

and continued wiping the mess from Jaya's sari into her own lap with a J-cloth. Jaya hated her for all this. She knew that if not for the crowd her mother would not even wipe a tear from her face.

"But, mom-", Jaya pleaded.

"Ju juss be quiet."

Jaya looked down at her ruined sari. She remembered it hanging in the window display at Radha's Sari Hut. It had never even been taken off the mannequin with that $999.99 price tag which it even had the audacity to boast: "Special Sale Price". Jari Vari, even. (Embroidered with beadwork and fine embossed needlework.) These were the saris that were laboured on by skilled Indian village trade workers who were probably paid less than thirty or maybe forty rupees per day. High profit. Low conscience.

Radha's display window, strategically located on the corner of 49th and Main in Vancouver's Little India, was easily viewable by passing cars. Cars that were held back by the traffic light were even able to make out the sales tags. Radha was a shrewd businesswoman, she had secured a market. Prestige and Pride were her best sellers. A laminated glossy cardboard sign with an "R" in the star logo in the left hand logo, stated in gold raised lettering: "This sari is now belonging to: _____." And, in bold, clear capital case letters, her eleven-year-old son would fill in the name of the purchaser which would then stay on display for the following week for everyone to see. A fine arrangement. No one complained. It was good for Radha's turnover, and it was good for women who wanted sari status. The people admired Radha for her wealth and power. Even her husband worked for her. And Radha's mannequins were the only ones that were all professionally airbrushed golden brown.

Jaya tried to make out Radha in the crowd of people sitting in fold out chairs in her living room. Her head was still spinning and she still had a few good heaves in her, but she did her best to hold them back. Most of the guests were invited out of obligation or in return for inviting Jaya's family to their weddings. This was her parents' wedding. Not hers. This is where favours were paid back, lives were changed, and grudges were buried.

Jaya's mother finished blotting what was left on the sari. The sour smell of milk gone off reminded her of the soggy cereal her mother had made her force down at breakfast. She held back another rise from her stomach. Jaya's mother put her fingers up to Jaya's mouth and forbade her to even think of getting sick again.

"Please, Jaya. Ju promised. No punny stuff." Jaya's mother put her head down and looked sadly into the lap of her sari. "No vedding, no money. Now stop looking so sick and smile for God's sake. Everybody's looking at ju."

"I am not doing this on purpose." Jaya whispered back.

Jaya's mother pretended to console her daughter, leaning over and patting her back saying: "If ju vant to go and shame this pamily's name, then ju juss keep it up young lady. Look at jore pather's face. He is going to hab a cardiac rest juss now. Now, sit up straight and try and look humble and pretty and put your head low. I vil go and rinse this, and Shastri vil iron my jellow sari pore ju and Nayla vil change jore lipstick."

Jaya's mother cradled the vomit-filled sari, while the others watched on, smiling nervously. Mother had successfully turned what might have been called an ill-omen or just plain disaster into a touching scene from a hit film. The guests oohed and ahhed and whispered amongst themselves with hands covering their mouths.

84

Jaya, the gold ornamented bride, sat motionless and stared into the swirly winding henna patterns on her feet. She could feel the eyes on her. The mud-like henna patterns looked so much better in dark brown than the orange-red color that would be left after rinsing the plant dye the following morning.

The stain in Jaya's dusty rose sari seemed to grow bigger every time she took notice of it. Her heart raced and her body trembled. An urgency grew within her. She knew her sari would be ready soon, and at any moment her mother would come to fetch her.

Discreetly and casually, Jaya leaned over to her cousin and whispered something into her ear. Her cousin turned to see if what she was hearing was correct, and then looked serious and unchanged and nodded her head. Jaya's mother had already slipped into a temporary *shalwar khameez* (Indian pant suit) and was mingling with the guests. Just at that moment, I watched as Jaya excused herself. "I will be right back" She motioned to anyone who might be looking. But the guests were all too busy talking amongst themselves. Some did take notice when she stood up, but Jaya presented them with a calm face that seemed to, in turn, calm them. Her strides were slow but confident.

I knew to follow her and meet her at the back door. When our eyes met, there was no need for any words to be exchanged. She just looked up at me, with tracks of mascara running down her cheeks and said, "What are you looking at? Let's go." Jaya did not turn back until she was more than half a block away. The house grew smaller and smaller and she smiled with each step imagining the stories they would tell. She walked and walked turning and laughing, the sari unravelling behind her – a trail of a memory soon to be forgotten.

Hot Papa

The children shout and dance as the train clunks past. The train does not go fast, but Hot Papa fears it anyway. He never let his own kids meet the train. Hot Papa knows that the locals think that this was because he didn't want them to mix with the blacks. And Hot Papa does not hire house servants, and he knows that the locals think that this is because he doesn't trust them in his home. Hot Papa eats dinner alone in the room across the chili fields and he knows that the locals think this is because he will not break a meal with them. And side-by-side they live and grow old together, with neither side ever knowing the truth.

Mama used to ask him all the time, especially after the birth of their youngest, Munira, "There is too much work for me. It is only to help with the girls. Yes? A little cooking, a little cleaning, and maybe a little sewing. Yes? Just 500 shillings a month, I'm sure we have –" But Hot Papa never let his wife finish. "It is not about money, Mama." Hot Papa has told her what it is about, but she argues adamantly. Mama says, "But they need the jobs. They need the money. They don't mind the dirty work or they wouldn't do it."

But Hot Papa doesn't mind the dirty work because it is his dirty work. When he tells Mama, "No one will do my dirty work but me," she calls him foolish and tells him that he might as well drink from the toilet water with the rest of them. But when Hot Papa makes the face she is silent. In twenty three years he has never laid a hand on his wife or his three daughters, and he knows he never will. He has, however, managed to master the face – and such a face – a face that commands silence even amidst the reddest of anger. But, Hot Papa is tired of the silence now. Everyday, Hot Papa walks the chili fields looking for noise.

Today, the sun is a crimson cherry egg nestled in a swirly mango pudding. Hot Papa paints the image in his mind. His hands are weak and cramped, but he dreams of painting the sun with the eight colour set of oils that his daughter sent from Uganda. He painted when Mama was in Dar-es-Salaam. He opened all the tubes and squirted small blobs of colour on the chili boxes because "canvas is too expensive for an amateur to waste". This is what Mama says. "When you get good, we will ask Salima to send canvas." But Hot Papa is good. He has never showed her his painting of Moyo because Mama will surely say that it doesn't look anything like Munira. "She's too dark! You don't remember our Muni, you old fool. Muni was white, white, like milk." Mama will not see what he sees. She will not see the faded blue jean hat, the pink wooden horse, or the swirly pudding in the sky. Mama will just see black.

Hot Papa keeps Moyo under the grass mat in Undali's drying station. Next time he will paint her smoother. He painted her with a chili and a chewed piece of sisal from Mama's basket because his daughter forgot to send a brush.

Hot Papa surveys the flatlands. It is too early for even the field workers, but not for the children. The children never get up this early for chores, only for the train. Their train. The Nairobi-Naivasha runs once a week at sunrise. It carries the people and the children's dreams to the big city. Hot Papa has stories of Nairobi, stories he is sure the children will enjoy, but stories he is sure the children will never hear. He walks towards the children, looking for Moyo, but when they see him coming they scatter like the black ants on the dry cracking mud that try to avoid his footsteps. Hot Papa can still see them in the distance, but he cannot hear them anymore.

Even over the loud hissing and dha-rhak, dha-rak of the train, Hot Papa hears them shouting and singing: *"Iko wapi Nairobi? Iko wapi?"* and the chorus of younger ones reply: *"Ipo pale, ipo pale, Nairobi, ipo pale,"* and point in the direction of the train's route to the big city. But as soon as they see the hot man coming toward them, they run. They do not know that he only wants to tell them stories about Nairobi Fair. They do not know that he only wants to tell them stories about the Nairobi street markets and the Colour Parade. They just run. Fast as their skinny legs can take them.

The sun peeks behind the painted Zofta sign just above the hill. The sign says: "Zofta. Available in three sizes." The mustard yellow paint is peeling and cracking from exposure to the relentless sun. The sign is meant for the train passengers, but the people of Naivasha want it to come down. It is ugly and old and it ruins the sunrise's attempt to start the day, they say. The baseboards of the Zofta sign show scars of attempted axe jobs. But behind the wood is a steel support bar. And so the sign stays.

What is this Zofta anyway? He has read the sign hundreds of times before without questioning it. Hot Papa had just accepted Zofta like the occasional pile of fly infested cow dung he would come across on the path that leads to the dairy farm—droppings of a runaway cow that won't get very far. You can't get far in Naivasha.

Hot Papa walks the footpath that divides his field into red chillies and green chillies. The colours are rich and strong and can be

88

seen from all the way up Old Naivasha Road, across the other side of the tracks. Hot Papa remembers when he only grew green chillies and sold them at the local market. And so his name: Hot Papa. *The hottest green chillies in Naivasha. So hot you can't even hold them. Hot Papa's chillies will burn holes through your fingers.* It was successful verbal marketing. No one ever stole from Hot Papa's fields because they feared the hot man. The locals said that his temper came from eating twenty to thirty chillies a day – with and without meals. One rumour made its way back to Hot Papa: *"He eats so many green chillies that he even shits green."*

This made Hot Papa laugh out loud. Sometimes the locals were crude. But when Mama heard this she screamed, "If you speak like them, you'll become like them." To which Hot Papa replied, "There is no them, Mama."

Nyekundu, Kijani. Red, Green. Hot Papa had to learn Swahili so that he could sell to the locals over the phone. They would take his chillies to the markets and the hotels up Kenyatta Avenue towards the Old Naivasha Road. They would order six pounds *nyekundu,* two pounds *kijani.* This is when Hot Papa had to replant his field. Times had gone and changed on him while he stayed pretty much the same. In the big city people had no time. They didn't want fresh green chillies anymore, they wanted dry red powder that they could store in glass jars in their cupboards. Nairobi wanted spoon spices. Quick and hot, not worked for. But Hot Papa never ate red. He liked the surprise of a fresh green chili. His bite would always be the same – half of the entire chili length regardless of size – but the chili wouldn't. Sometimes the chili would be any empty bullet, a weak taste of green, and other days the surge would force him to hiccup and cough, almost painfully, and Hot Papa would always say, "Good, good."

But, no one had time for surprises anymore.

It wasn't long before Hot Papa's field divided itself in response to the needs of the people. The green chili plants started to burn and dry out in the hot sun, and the picked chillies that Hot Papa stored in rice sacks in the shade behind his house were fast rotting. Hot Papa planted red chillies where the green chillies once grew. He had to hire three of the locals to help him pick, dry and crush them into a fine red powder. He paid them good money and though they hardly spoke a word, they were silent friends. The locals made fun of the three workers and called them traitors. They were caught in the middle. They worked in Hot Papa's chili fields and made good money, but back home, on the other side of the tracks, they were mocked for siding with the hot man. No matter how they spoke of Hot Papa's gentle ways and generosity, the locals stood their ground. So the workers lived on one side of the tracks and worked on the other, but felt like the train— just passing through.

Mama always said, "You are a fool. You are just making more work for yourself." It was only when the red side of the field began to spread alongside the train tracks like trail weed that Mama said: "I suppose it is a good thing." But then again, Mama is still bitter about the pink horse.

In the distance Hot Papa sees Moyo – it is not her real name of course, but it is the name Hot Papa has given her since she was afraid to give her own. She is only six, but she is as tall as some of the ten year olds. He waves at her, but she doesn't see him. One of the older boys spots Hot Papa's hand the turns and starts running towards the mud shacks with his little sister trailing behind. The other children look back and forth from Hot Papa to the running two. They stand hesitantly. Watching their own. Looking for warning signs like alert impalas, listening for rustling in the dry yellow grass. Hot Papa starts to walk back towards the house. His daily walk gets shorter and shorter as the years go by.

"Undali!" Hot Papa walks slowly, picking a few of the burnt chillies along the way and letting them fail to the ground. Undali comes running out to meet Hot Papa in the fields. He is the only one of the three workers left. The other two moved to Nairobi for more work. Hot Papa knows that when he dies he will leave the field to Undali. Mama will be fine with Shamshir and her husband in Dar-es-Salaam, and Salima and her husband are doing well in Uganda. Hot Papa knows that Mama will not care for the fields. Mama will like living in Dar-es-Salaam. She won't miss the chili field.

"Yes?" Undali reaches out to hold Hot Papa's arm.

"No, please, I am fine."

Undali walks slow to match Hot Papa's pace. "Is there some trouble?"

"No. No trouble. Just ... just the train."

"Yes, Hot Papa ... the train." Undali points to the tracks and nods his head.

"The train must ... must ..." Hot Papa pauses beside the stack of chili baskets to catch his breath. He fans his hand in front of his chest as if trying to quicken the air's route to his lungs. He points to the house. "I can't talk and walk," he says.

Undali walks with him to the house. Mama comes out and asks, "Is everything okay?"

"Yes, Mama." Undali says.

Hot Papa sits on the chair that looks out to the fields while Undali kneels beside him.

"Would you like some water, Papa? Mama says.

Undali looks up at Mama and smiles. "Hot Papa is still a strong man, yes?"

"Yes." She says and looks at Hot Papa who is looking down into his lap. "Papa," she says loudly as if he is having trouble hearing her, "would you like some water?"

"Yes," Hot Papa leans over the chair and looks at her, "we would, thank you."

Mama glances at him, just on the edge of speaking, but she says nothing and comes back minutes later with two glasses.

"The train, Hot Papa?" Undali looks up at Hot Papa who is motioning for him to sit on the chair beside him.

"The train must stop."

"Papa, stop this *buk-buk*," Mama blurts out. Undali looks back, surprised to find her standing at the door listening. "You've been saying this for days now." Mama walks back into the house.

"Stop?" Undali looks at Hot Papa who appears to be smiling faintly. "But, Hot Papa, this is impossible, the Naivasha-Nairobi must run. It has stayed –"

"Hush, hush, now. Pass me the water. I said this to get rid of Mama." Hot Papa wheezes softly. "She thinks I'm fading away, you know? *Pagla*!" Hot Papa points to his head.

"Oh, Mama, yes. She doesn't like me much."

"Me neither."

They both laughed and sipped on the water.

"Mine's warm," says Hot Papa.

Mine's cold," says Undali. "I must have got yours!"

"Oh she is a bitter woman." Hot Papa pours his water over his toes. He wiggles his toes and has a sip from Undali's glass and passes it back to him.

"But you were going to say something about the train."

"Yes. Yes...I was." Hot Papa looks across the tracks and points from the beginning of the tracks to as far as he can see them. "We need to build a fence."

"What?"

"A fence."

"A fence, Hot Papa?" Undali looks confused.

"Yes. Yes, a fence." Hot Papa coughs and spits to the side. "A wire fence ... like that one." Hot Papa points to the chicken fence just outside the dairy farm.

"No one will steal the chillies, Hot Papa, I will make sure." Undali smiles a big white toothy grin. It reminds Hot Papa of the time that he hired him. Undali was just a teenager sitting on the other side of the tracks raking the dry grass for cow feed. Hot Papa asked the boy if he would like to work on the chili fields with him. Undali smiled big. But now Undali has grey hair that sits like a halo around his head. He is balding in the centre. Hot Papa is glad his own hair is almost all gone. He would much rather be bald than balding.

"It is not the chillies I'm worried about. I'm worried about the children. They're always coming so close and –"

"Oh no, Hot Papa, it just looks close, they're just having fun. The children wait for Thursdays. It's just fun." Undali looks towards the tracks.

"Fun? Don't tell me about fun, Undali, I lost my Munira to that train."

Undali looks away in the direction of the Zofta sign. He knows that Munira was not lost to the train. He knows the real story, and he knows it is more painful.

"Yes. I am sorry, Hot Papa."

"Yes." Hot Papa nods. "I was thinking to make one along both sides of the track for at least twice the length of the fields. Just to be safe, yes?"

"Yes, Hot Papa." Undali follows Hot Papa's stare to the tracks. "And what if the children run to the end of the fence to greet the train?"

"Well that is where we will have to sit."

Undali's face tenses. "We will sit?"

Hot Papa nods and pours some water in his hand and rubs it on his scalp and motions to pour some in Undali's hands and Undali does the same.

"Every Thursday." Hot Papa says and smiles at the mastery of his plan.

Undali rubs his forehead in small tight circles. "But –"

"Just until the train has safely passed. For our children."

Undali looks out towards the chili fields. "And what about the chillies?"

"The chillies are not children, Undali. They don't dance and sing for the train. Muni did. She said she wanted to go places. She said she wanted to go fast like the train."

"Yes, Papa." Undali looks at the tears that form in Hot Papa's eyes. His breaths are shorter and quicker now. Undali leans forward to listen so that Hot Papa does not have to strain.

"She looked like one of the young children that dances for the trains now. Moyo, I call her. You've seen her?"

Undali shakes his head slowly, "I don't know."

"Munira wanted to run over that hill there, see?" Hot Papa points to where the black tracks disappear.

Undali looks at the hill and remembers Munira's story.

The parade was one of Nairobi's biggest. Red, violet, and yellow streamers decorated the streets. The people stood together despite the previous week's riots. Kenyatta Day's celebrations drowned all the sorrows into a sea of music and food and vibrations. The drums vibrated so loudly that the people felt it in their veins. They moved to the music unconsciously. Swaying in and out of the beat lik instruments in a tune.

"She wanted to run as fast as the train. She thought that it c right through the hills." Hot Papa wipes his forehead. "That's wher bought her the horse. I thought it might get her mind off the train. B it didn't.

95

The dancers jerked to the rhythm in sync. They teased the onlookers by tripping and falling and pretending to be hurt. The other dancers would huddle around the injured one like elephants around the young. The music would start to fade as the musicians noticed the problem. The performers would play along for awhile. The crowd would begin to panic and the injured one would leap up and begin dancing again. The crowd would cheer. Munira didn't understand. "Is he dead?" She would say. Even after the third time.

"I found the wooden horse in Tanzania. I had gone for three days, you remember? It was quite a lot of money, but I told the shop owner that I could supply him with as much chili powder as he liked. Well he laughed at me. Hard. I wanted to smack him. I knew that the price of the wooden horse would probably mean two years of chili. I'm not stupid. Everyone needs chili, right?"

The crowd watched as the parade fell before them. Each act would top the previous one. Jugglers, fire dancers, bubble makers, human pyramids, and all kinds of bicycle tricks. Undali had only been to one parade before. All it had was a float with musicians and a few dancers. It couldn't compare. He was grateful to Hot Papa for inviting him to come along while Mama and the other two workers stayed behind to guard the chili fields. But the locals warned him that there would be trouble. They said that Hot Papa was up to no good. Even his wife said that she dreamed of trouble the night before. Undali didn't know that the villagers could be right and wrong at the same time.

"Well finally he agreed, but he made me feel like a monkey. He made me feel like I was begging for the horse. Which I guess I was in a way. But he knew I wasn't going to ride the damn thing. He knew it was for my Muni. But he didn't have any kids. So maybe he really didn't understand. I guess that's why. But when I told him about the train he seemed to understand the urgency. He said that he had been on the Nairobi-Naivasha before. He got sick on it."

It all happened in a second. Hot Papa had told Undali to hold Salima's hand while he picked up Muni. She was tired of the noise. She was crying, but her sounds could barely be heard over the bass. Her mouth opened and closed and the tears fell endlessly. Undali remembered the faces he made at her. Faces that always made her laugh. He remembered thinking, "With all those tears filling up her eyes, everything must be blurry." And then, "Jihadhari!" the man's voice came from behind, "Look out!" Undali had pulled Salima out of the way and yelled at Hot Papa to move. And that's when the fire broke. The fire from his costume caught the ends of Muni's hair. As soon as the heat reached Hot Papa's arm, he dropped her. Undali rushed to them and threw his jacket over Muni's head, but the fire was spreading fast, and the more he patted it the more it grew. Hot Papa stood back and watched in horror. He stood pressing Salima's head into his stomach. All he kept saying was, "This is not the way. This is not the way."

"It was beautiful though. Worth feeling like a monkey. Somehow, when I carried it to the car, I knew. I knew Muni would ride it all day. She would pull on its white rope and ride as far as her imagination would take her. She would braid its yellow ribbons and wash it in the chili fields. Muni would be happy with this horse. She would put on her jean hat and ride it beside the train. I imagined the noise of the train in her head. I thought she would just ride alongside it." Hot Papa wipes his eyes and looks out into the fields.

At first some of the people paid no attention. Some even laughed while others looked closer – amazed at the realistic effects. Part of the act. Everybody but the dancers thought it was part of the act. One by one the dancers ran to Muni, trying to stop the flames. They waved their hands violently at the crowd to make room for the ambulance to come through. But it was the people that prevented the ambulance from reaching on time. The sirens blended into the music until finally it was just the sirens. Hot Papa rocked back and forth, clutching Salima. "This is not the way, no, no, no, this is not, no, no –"

"That's Moyo there, see?"

Undali looks up at Hot Papa who is staring blankly across the tracks at something beyond.

"Can you see? In the hat. See?"

Undali spots the young girl in the distance. Undali is surprised to see that Hot Papa can see this far. "I think she's waving at you."

Hot Papa waves big with his hands. "She has the wooden horse now. Mama was sore with me. She wanted to save it. God knows why." Hot Papa gets up and stands. Moyo turns around and walks further away, into the village on the other side of the tracks. "She rides it sometimes, but I think she is getting tired of it."

Undali looks up at Hot Papa who is still watching Moyo. "There is wire at Amasa's farm across the tracks. I will bring some back tomorrow."

"We won't need some Undali. We will need lots."

An Elephant Never Charges

Juma walks up the footpath towards me. He is twenty minutes late. I watch him walk and I realize that this is one of the things I love most about him. Juma lets his arms hang heavy and sway from side to side like a gorilla. But Juma is almost six feet and he only weighs 48 kilos. *"A slim gorilla,"* I smile.

Today, his chest is heaved forward, but some days he forgets and lets his back arch naturally. He struts slowly towards me. I forget waiting and sweating in the hot sun because he is carrying two sticks of sugar cane and a small bag of apples which I know he has stolen from Mkoti market. Juma is wearing his "love shirt". This is what I call it, anyway. It is khaki with a black button line down the front and black on the hem of the short sleeves. The buttons are the same khaki material held in by a gold band.

Juma doesn't even slow down when he gets to me. He continues up the footpath in the wrong direction, towards Umbeze trail, and doesn't even check to see if I am following.

"Tunakwenda Manda." Juma says, finally.

"Manda?! But I thought we were going to—"

"I know. But I changed my mind. Today, we are going to Manda." Juma continues walking.

"You can't just change your mind, Juma. Besides, I don't want to go to Manda." I try my best not to sound scared.

"Why?" Juma stops and turns around to look at me. "You scared?" He laughs and continues towards the mangrove swamps.

"Don't be silly, Juma. I'm not even wearing the right pair of shoes." I regret saying this seconds after the words have left my mouth.

"Oh-ho, and how many pairs do you have, my dear Chum-Chum?"

Juma calls me this. We are Masai and Chum-Chum to his friends. He is Masai, the tall, lean, black warrior, and I am Chum-Chum, the short, stout, green-eyed Indian film star, known on TV commercials for her long-lasting, breath-freshening, mango-flavoured Chum-Chum chewing gum. It's his nickname for me. He always smiles when he says it; but I am still not sure if I like it, just the same.

Juma knows me. But, this time he is wrong. I am scared of the stories, not the island itself. Some say Manda is even more spectacular than Zanzibar. And I have seen pictures. Manda sunsets are a must on all the tourists' lists. The skies change color so quickly on Manda, and noone seems to know why. Some of the elders say that once you are on the island, you are in a different place, with a different sky.

Once, my father brought back a series of thirty-six Manda pictures that were taken on the automatic timer—frame by frame—one every sixty seconds. That night, he was so excited that he developed them himself instead of waiting for *"Jamal's Foto Foto"* to open the

100

next morning. He called me into the dark room with him. We didn't say a word as the single shadowed baobab tree came up again and again in the tray, but each time with a different sun-coloured backdrop. Soft swirls of creamy mango, blush watermelon, pink passion fruit, cherry maroon, and banana yellow—and all of these colors in just over half an hour. My father swore that he did not notice it while it was happening because the whole sky would just change so suddenly, "as if in the half-second blink of an eye."

My father took pictures on the island just before he died. He was very good and the tourists would pay big shillings for his pictures. They would even ask for him by name. Many of the hotels on the coast of Mombasa knew Dhanesh. Some of the tourists would even ask the hotel managers to leave messages for him at the desk. And my father would walk up and down the coast collecting business like crabs in his net. He was charming and could capture any emotion in seconds with the lens of his camera.

Juma hands me a sugar cane. It smells faintly of shoe polish. I tear a piece of the flesh off with my teeth and suck the juices out. It is sweeter than the local kind. The Mkoti market hand picks their fruits and vegetables especially for the rich tourists. The mangoes are a dark, rich orange, cut by the vendors into flower petals, with sprinkles of *pili-pili* (chili pepper) and rock salt, the corn is barbecued over coals in its husk, the papaya and guava are balled and served in watermelon bowls with custard and condensed milk, and the passion fruit cups and pineapple wedges are displayed in banana leaf trays next to the exotic coconut shell cocktails and fresh juices.

"Did you steal these?" But I am enjoying the cane too much to really care.

"Of course not," Juma smiles, "I sold my bike and paid for them."

"You'll get caught one day, you know. You'll lose your job."

"I've tried." Juma kicks at a stone and misses. "If only I could be so lucky." Juma speaks like the tourists. He makes a face and spits out a dry piece of cane and bites off another.

"Why do you hate it so much? It's a good job, and you get to meet all the foreigners." I say and hand Juma my cane to trade for his.

"Oh, and how about your mother, my Chum-Chum, do you think she will say the same about my profession." He hands me his cane and takes mine.

Playfully, I reach back and grab my cane back and switch them quickly from hand to hand. "And why should you care what my mother thinks? You are not in love with me are you?"

Juma just shakes his head and walks faster up the trail. I catch up to him and offer both sticks of sugar cane. "Here. You pick. Whoever gets the sweet one gets the sweet one, and whoever gets the bitter, can't complain, yes?"

Juma turns to face me and fans a fly away from my face, "Oh, you are such a foolish little girl with a head full of dreams, Halima. I am no more in love with you than I am with polishing shoes, so you just keep walking with a little less talking, okay?"

I offer both canes again, but he motions with his hands that I can have both. So, I do.

We play love games, Juma and I. This is what I like to think. I have been in love with Juma ever since my father introduced him to me.

Juma didn't treat me like the other boys, smiling and winking at me when my father's back was turned; Juma paid absolutely no attention to me whatsoever.

The day we met, the streets were buzzing with excitement and flooded with colour. Men put away their drab white t-shirts and the women chose bright red, orange, yellow and green *kitenges* (loose flowing dresses) with flowers, wild animal prints and African landscapes. Framed pictures of Daniel Arap Moi were displayed in the front window of every store instead of in the back by the cash register or above the door frame at the entrance. The President had finally called off his dogs—the Kanu Youth Brigade—and the people rejoiced and praised Moi's name in public, trusting that his plainclothes guards might report it back to him. And Moi probably smiled, looking forward to the evening television programming of his face on all the channels, declaring peace... for the time being.

"Halima, this is Juma, the shoe-shiner." My father yelled above the locals singing and playing music in the streets. "You know. The Nikon. The zoom lens?"

I pretended not to remember, hoping my father might lengthen the introduction.

"Oh, come on, Halima. I told you about him. Juma, you know, the shoe-shiner that gave me the tip about the German's zoom lens? I'm sure I told you."

Of course he told me. Every time he showed me a zoom shot of his that he was proud of, he told me: the close-up of the gazelle's eyes, scared and tense, the sun setting its melting colours on the waves, the lean lioness pose stalking, just before the chase, the mother giraffe lowering its neck tenderly down to the newborn to feed it leaves from the tall trees. My father's face was electric. But how could he have known that this one introduction might probably change the rest of my life.

Juma is a few steps ahead of me now. I drop the rest of my sugar cane and wipe my hands on the back of my skirt.

"So, did you miss me, my Masai?" I reach for his hand.

Juma turns and pretends to look at the other side of the road before crossing, not letting go of my hand, as if checking for a bike or Land Rover. But I know he is smiling. Hardly anyone takes these roads except by foot or bicycle—and even if someone was coming, we would have heard the tires on the gravel long before they were close enough to hit us.

The sky is clearing now, the clouds parting just for Juma and me. The sun beats down even harder on our backs. I put my hand on my head. My hair is burning hot. Juma tells me that it won't be long before we reach the coast.

"Then you can put some of the Indian Ocean on your Indian head." He says. His front tooth is chipped, but it makes his smile even that much more charming. When Juma chews gum, he forms a small piece of the gum to correct the chip and then smiles at me and says, "Now, does this make me look more handsome?" And I always tell him, "No."

The sweat makes my new cotton dress stick to my chest, but Juma has not noticed, yet. Every few minutes I slap at my skirt to shake the powder red dirt that is lining it from the road. Juma's knees are dry and dusty compared to the rest of his black, smooth body. He hands me the bag of apples.

"Find the coolest one, Chum-Chum—in the middle."

Reaching into the back pocket of his shorts, Juma pulls out his "Jackie". A rich English tourist gave it to him last week for shining his shoes. He misplaced his wallet and didn't have any money on him so he gave up his Swiss Army Knife. "Will you take my 'Jackie' for the shine?" is what he said. When Juma tells the story he does the accent.

Normally, Juma gets upset at the tourists. Some of them leave it to the last minute to tell him that they don't have any money on them. Sometimes he gets stuck with a pen, or an old notebook, but every now and again he gets a deal. This Jackie replaced Juma's old pocket knife real quick. It had a bottle opener, two knives, a spoon, a nail-cutter, a pair of scissors and a fancy "J" engraved on it. Juma thought it might be the first letter of the man's name, or that maybe the brand name of the knife was "Jackie". But, Juma didn't care. It was his now, and as far as he was concerned, the "J" was for Juma.

Juma pulled out the longest knife and began cutting the apple, letting the curvy peelings fall behind us as we walked.

"Why Manda?" I ask him finally.

"To see the umbuyu trees." Juma says.

"All the way to Manda for umbuyus? Look there." I point to a tall dark baobab in the dry grasses in the distance. "What's wrong with that one?"

"The umbuyu stand in a straight line on Manda near the Takwa ruins. It's supposed to be a very special sacred place, Halima." Juma looks at me and tucks a loose hair behind my ear, "And anyway, don't you think it's about time you got over your fears. Come on, this will be good for you."

I walk towards the water even though inside I don't want to; each and every step filled with guilt. Ever since my father died in Manda, I swore to my mother that I would never visit the famous island. I used to think that she made me swear this out of respect to a silly superstition. When I asked her why she made me promise she would say, "You can visit the dead person's place of rest, but not the place of the death."

Although my mother told me that my father was killed by an elephant on Manda, the villagers all tell different versions. Sometimes when I am walking with Juma, I can hear them talking to each other. "Oho! Isn't she the daughter of the dead Dhanesh—the photographer who was taken by the Manda Spirits?" And then the response would come, "You mean that Hindu man who married that Muslim wife?" "Yes, they say he was killed while trying to take a picture of an elephant." "But he be taking picture of many animal and he would have never gone too close for it to charge." "Yes, but this is what they say." "Maybe they say this to protect the girl." "Yes, yes. Maybe to protect the girl."

I have believed my mother for years and only recently have I started having doubts as to what actually took place. Sometimes the details of the story change. Small details—the kind that someone who doubts would notice.

I work full time, now, at the Kasori Market to help support my mother since my father is gone. We live with my Uncle, my father's brother and he is young and not as yet married so the villagers talk even more. Some of them even come right up to me and gossip about my father, and so his death continues.

"Babies. Babies them harder to shoot than bigger elephants." Nyaharu, the village mother came and told me one day. "They jus' keep movin' an' cryin'. Can't take no good pictures of them. Jus' s'pposed to remember them in the head. Ask me I know." Nyaharu has seven children, all under fourteen years old. She thinks she knows everything. "You jus' go an' watch the elephant. They a kind, kind animal. Them more scare of us people then we be of them. I telling you. This story your Mama be telling you is a no good. No good. She a good woman, yes, but she gone an' done a bad thing. She gone an' marry a wrong man. God done and say all Hindu marry a Hindu an' all Muslim s'pposed to marry a Muslim. But when a Muslim marry a Hindu—watch out! That when trouble be comin' a lookin' for you. I telling you, Hali, your father ain't been charged by no elephant. Them Spirits in Manda gone and get him."

When Nyaharu told me this I couldn't stop myself from crying. When I reached home I questioned my mother for details. I knew it would be hard for her but I needed to know.

"Did he get too close, Mama?" I asked her. "Please tell me."

"We don't know, Halima." My mother said. "Some think he might have been taking a picture of a baby elephant and the mother was nearby."

"So now it's a baby elephant?" I was getting frustrated. More details.

"We don't know for sure."

"So what do we know for sure?"

"That your father was a good man, Halima." She looked harshly at me. "And that's all we need to know."

"Ma, you know that Papa is not stupid. He would never go to close to a mother and baby elephant. He would just never do such a thing."

"Maybe he didn't see the mother." Mother looked into her lap as if remembering something.

"Papa would never go to close to a baby. He would know that the mother would be nearby. Everyone knows that a baby never wanders far from its mother." I said. And how do you know it was an elephant anyway? The camera was damaged and we have no pictures of what he took last."

"Oh, Halima, you know how. The way the body was discovered." Mother made a face and looked like she was recalling the details in her head. "It had to be something very powerful and big. You know that there is no way any human could have done—Oh, Halima, why do you do this to me over and over again?"

"So? Who says it had to be an elephant?"

"What else could it be?" Mother looked me right in the eyes. "Who's been telling you things, Halima?"

"Nobody. Why? Should they be? Maybe they'll tell me the things that you are not!"

Mother started to pace the floor. She undid the bun in her hair, and with her fingers she combed through some of the knots.

"Why do you listen to them? They are full of garbage talk. That is all they do. They are bored and they have nothing better to do than make up stories to pass the time." Mother walked over to me and sat down beside me. In one move she wound her hair into a bun again. "We only have what we know. Now, you shouldn't ask so many questions or your father's soul will not be at rest. You should pray for him." Mother turned away from me.

I got up from the chair. "And where should I pray? At the mosque or the temple?" I snapped at her.

"Halima, please don't be so cruel to me. I am sorry that he died—"

"I thought you said he was killed."

"Hali, please. God can hear all good prayers." Mother started to cry. "Just pray for him in any language. In your heart, whenever you think of him. I am sure He will hear you." Mother walked out of the kitchen sobbing, leaving me with more questions than I had to begin with.

* * * * * *

The waters rush the coastline and I am already thinking of ways to back out of going, but Juma looks determined and I know I will be safe with him. There are many dhow captains looking our way, each one hoping that we will choose their boat. Some of them climb to the top of their lookouts to get our attention, while other shout out: "*Namaste, As-Salaam Wa Alay Khum, and Kaise Hai?*" They try all the languages, hoping to get my attention. I know they think that I am a rich tourist and Juma is just my guide. Juma is angry at their assumptions. He yells back in Swahili: "*Una alisema sana!*" Immediately they realize that we are locals and possibly even a couple.

"So?" Juma looks at me with a concerned look on his face.

"So, what?"

"You haven't said a word the whole way here. Are you mad at me for bringing you here?" Juma holds out his hand and helps me down the slope to the beach. I notice that the coast is almost completely empty. No tourists, no snack sellers, no postcard vendors, no nothing. Most of the tourists stay indoors when the sun is at its hottest. But it is the twelfth of December, a day for celebration with or without shade.

"I'm not mad, Juma. I just don't know if I am ready."

"I know. You're scared. But you shouldn't be, Chum-Chum. I am with you." Juma looks at all the captains as we walk past them and dips his hand in the cool clear blue water and puts some on my head. "This will be good for you. Many people go to Manda and leave all their worries there. You will see."

Juma picks a captain and walks out to the dhow while I wait on the shore. I tell him that I am not even going near the boat until it is absolutely clear that we can return by seven. "I trust you." I tell him. "It's the winds that I am worried about." He knows that my curfew is normally six so he doesn't even attempt to sway me.

They talk and point for a bit while I watch. The captain looks concerned until Juma takes something shiny out of his back pocket. He looks at the shiny rock and places it to his mouth as if tasting it. And then with a nod, he puts it in his bag and they both wave at me to come and join them.

I make my way when suddenly one dhow captain shouts to me, "Hey! Miss Bombay! You tell your boy that I will take you across for fifty shillings less than that guy!" Fortunately, for him, Juma didn't hear a word he said. The waves rock the dhows in unison, and they creak and sway—dancing to the rhythm of the ocean.

The boats rely completely on the skill of the captain and the wind, this much I know. I have never been on a dhow, but I won't tell Juma this. I look at the boat and it seems sturdy and secure enough. It is a simple four person wooden boat with a raised sail and a small lookout. The wood is thin and lacquered. The boats are rarely painted for fear that on longer journeys, should the wind trap the boat in the sun's sharp rays the paint might melt and burn the passengers. On either side of the dhow is an extended bar float so that when the captain climbs to the lookout, the boat remains steady. A small ringed cone flag hangs from the top of the dhow so that the captain can keep track of the wind's direction and force.

"Come on, Halima. I'll help you in. Give me your hand." Juma is excited about our journey and I do not want to disappoint him.

"But they can be so unreliable, Juma. I've heard of a dhow that was caught in the Ocean for seventeen hours—"

"Oh, Chum-Chum, you know that's not going to happen. Look at the day. It is clear and there isn't even any boat traffic. It's just beautiful, Hali. While everyone's eating fancy meals at expensive restaurants and hotels and drinking expensive wine, we can celebrate Independence Day the way it should be celebrated." Juma is so excited and convincing.

"And what way is that?"

"Together, of course." He reaches out his hand to me and I can't help but walk towards him. "The captain's name is Madison and he has promised me we will be back in plenty of time for me to return you home on time."

When Madison sees that I am coming, he jumps up with excitement and waves. The other dhow captains look on in envy. They know that the tourists won't come out for a while. And when they do, many will not want to make the entire trip to Manda, but rather just experience a short sail on the boat and turn back. The night would promise many more festivities and fireworks for Kenya's Independence and the memory of Jomo Kenyatta—the man responsible.

As we near the boat, Juma turns to me and whispers, "Are you wearing anything under there?"

"Why?" I slap his hand away. "How rude, Juma!"

"No. The boat, you *mbuzi*. The dhow. You have to walk in the water a bit to get in. Just a bit, don't worry, I'll hold you." Juma says. "You'll be okay, I promise. But I don't think the same can be said for this." Juma waves the lace hem of my new white skirt in the air.

Just then, the same dhow captain that called out before whistles and yells, "Hey, hey! Miss Bombay! You can do it!"

Before I realize how I angry I am I yell back suddenly, "Urray, Mr. Congo! I am just fine so you just wait for Miss Bombay. I am Miss Kenya. *Mzuri. Hakuna ma tata.* Okay? You got it!"

Juma looks at me surprised and just starts laughing, "So, my little Chum-Chum is now Miss Kenya, yes?" He picks me up and carries me to the boat and places me in, while I just sit at one side and ring out the end of my skirt paying no attention to the other captains.

Madison looks older and more experienced than the others somehow. He is a slender black man of about fifty years with salt and pepper hair. His eyes are small and deep set and when he squints in the sun it looks as if they are closed. He hands me a towel and it is then that I notice he is missing three fingers on his right hand. I wonder what might have caused this, but the dhow has no motor. I realize I must have been looking too long when he says, "You no need worry, madam. Everything okay."

For the rest of the trip I make a conscious effort not to look anywhere near his hand, but this is not easy. Juma is unfastening the anchor and Madison hands me the rope ends to tie. I glance, just for a second, at the three stub knuckles and puckered flesh while trying to keeping my face expressionless.

"Madam, you no worry." He points to his hand. "If you want I can tell you. It is no problem. You no worry. Is okay, really."

I look up at his small eyes. But when they meet mine, I look away.

Madison pushes us out of the shallow end and the boat wobbles back and forth, while the waves slap against the sides. The air is much cooler on the water. I look up at the cone sail. Wind.

The wood is hot under me so I take the wet part of my skirt and dampen it. But this only cools it for a few minutes before the sun has dried it again. Juma watches me from the other side and smiles. I wish that he would come and sit beside me instead of making small talk with Madison about starting up his own business, sailing and the rains.

Madison throws me a towel and tells me to hang it over the edge of the boat and soak it with cool water for my head. Juma asks him endless questions and before long I let their chatter fade into the background and let the mist spray my face. I rest my head on the towel and let my eyes close and the swaying of the boat and the flap-flapping of the wind through the cone sail lulls me to sleep.

"You really are such a sleeping beauty." I wake up to Juma stroking my hair. "Such beautiful hair, you have a curtain of black silk."

"Juma?" I squint at Juma in the sun.

"We're almost there. You should get up now so you can see the island."

"No." I get up and look. The island is huge and we are so close. The waters crash against the white beach and the sand sparkles like diamonds in the sun. I feel nauseous and dizzy.

Madison, who is perched on the lookout, turns to look down at us now that our voices are raised enough to reach him over the winds. When he sees me, he smiles innocently and says, "Welcome to Manda, Madam. I told you. Everything be okay."

"Juma, I don't think I can do this. This is the island that took my father." My hands are trembling and my stomach turning.

"But Halima, look at it. This is where you will get peace. Your father is gone now, but this is where he was last. I really thought this would help you." Juma stares back in the direction of the coast. But it is just miles and miles of turquoise water now.

I look towards the island. It looks peaceful enough. The trees are swaying gently, and the beach looks so clean without so many people littered all over it. Manda has no real tourist industry. Maybe the locals made up the story about the Manda Spirits just to protect themselves from the real scavengers. In school they taught us that back in the sixteenth century, the entire Swahili Village just picked up and left Takwa and moved to Lamu. No one knows why. Not even the history books. And so it is that people come to see the vacant city, but they rarely stay the night. And that's where Madison, Mr. Congo and the others come in. They make a healthy profit just going back and forth for the curious tourists, and that's pretty much all there is to it.

The Takwa ruins still live. But some say, so too do the Spirits. Even some travel books warn the visitors to be wary. And so Manda sacrifices the industry to Lamu. Tourists looking for sun, vendors looking for tourists, locals looking for stories and everyone looking for something. But no one remembering the day. December 12, 1963. The day Kenya was really born. I tie my hair into a bun like my mother's and I don't notice Juma behind me until he unties it and lets it fall down my back.

"I'm sorry, Halima." He says. So sweet and soft. Nothing else. No excuses.

When I don't answer or even turn to face him, he says it even louder and more sincerely.

"I was an idiot. I really thought this might help you in some way. Of course you would have trouble coming here." Juma takes my hand in his and I turn to face him. "Please, Halima. Forgive me. I'll tell Madison to take us back and we can just enjoy the sail back, okay? I am really sorry. But this time no sleeping, yes?" Juma is trying to smile.

"No, Juma." I feel the heat in my cheeks and tears start to form in my eyes, but I don't let them fall. "I am ready for this now. I want to see the island that took my Papa.

"Are you sure?" Juma asks.

I picture Madison sighing and readjusting the sail to catch the wind back home.

"Yes." I say, taking his hand in mine. "I must do this. This is where he came last."

Madison's t-shirt is stained with dark patches of sweat under his arms and an oval in the middle of his chest. He climbs down from the lookout and dips a straw hat into the water and places it on his head. The water drips down in beads down his face. The wind has settled and we are at least twenty feet from the shore. He passes Juma a pole, and together they guide the dhow to the coastline. Madison steadies the dhow and walks towards me.

"I am sorry about your father, Madam."

I resent him for listening, but at the same time admire him for his honesty. His small grey eyes are genuine and filled with such kindness. He reaches out to shake my hand and I feel his thumb and finger wrap around my hand. His stubs grip slightly but firmly, just enough to say they are there.

"Now, you two be careful there. You must stay together and I come and pick you in one hour for trip back. Winds be good. I feel in the sky. Little cloud is better, and winds good for going home. You no worry, I be right here." Madison looks over my head and yells to Juma. "No more, no more. Close enough. Too many rocks here. Is okay now."

"Thank you, Madison."

"No, thank you, Madam." Juma looks at his hand. "You first person to touch my hand. I always shake with left so nobody have to touch me. Since motor do this, I sail the dhow." He pats the side of the boat like a dog, and splashes more water on his face with his hat. "No more fast boat. Better to trust wind. Is better, no?"

"Yes, Madison. Better to trust the wind." I say.

Juma hops out of the dhow and holds it steady for me and I let my skirt get wet at the ends. I put my shoes on when I get to the sand which is so soft and white, but too hot to walk on. The beach is not as empty as it looked from the water. There are people walking back and forth, some locals, some tourists. And there aren't as many snack vendors as there are on the coast, but I can smell barbequed fish, and corn and mogo in the air. I look back at Juma who is giving Madison some money and at Madison who is blowing on a harmonica and smiling at the sounds it makes from one end to the other.

White sand sticks to the wet ring of my skirt as we walk to the road. A Black Muslim woman sits in the shade of a tree weaving a sisal basket while a young baby sleeps beside her. She is wearing a faded blue dress with short sleeves and her body is lean and strong. I try to imagine how such a woman could have given birth to such a plump and healthy baby. I become more aware of my own body. I suck in my stomach and try to walk tall. But it is hopeless because I look even shorter and chubbier next to Juma. I picture Miss. Chum-Chum chewing the orange gum on TV. The woman looks up from her weaving and smiles at us.

Juma's steps are slow as we walk towards the sign for the Takwa ruins. Putting his arm around my back he asks if I am okay. I nod, but I am not ready to speak. There is too much in my heart and too much to see. I stare blankly at the limestone and coral houses. Their color is brilliant despite their age, and intensified by the sun that filters through the trees.

I look at the tall trees, all in a line, and walk hand in hand with Juma on the sands of the island that took my father. Juma sits down resting his head against the trunk of a great tree and I lay my head in his lap. Within minutes he is asleep. I reach into his pocket for his Jackie and make the only offering I can think of to my father.

I unfold the scissors and watch as my thick hair falls in bits, and blows away in the gentle Manda breeze.

Celebrating
African American Marriages

Annie Rivers

DEDICATION

This book is dedicated to my parents, my daddy, Mr. Taylor J. Wimberly who passed away on February 27, 2004, and to my mother Ms. Creasey Farrar Wimberly. My mother gives me a cup of inspiration whenever I need it. She is a phenomenal woman who has overcome many challenges in life. She is truly the wind beneath my wings and I love her very much....and to my two daughters Crystal and Cherie, their daddy Henry who passed away December 12, 2006. The three of them have taught me how to love unconditionally. I am thankful for the young accomplished African American women they have become, truly a gift from God.

Love and Blessings Always.

ACKNOWLEDGMENTS

I would like to take this opportunity to express my sincere appreciation to all that assisted in completing this book. I give all praise and glory to my Lord and Savior, Jesus Christ for giving me strength and guidance during this journey.

Second, I would like to thank all of the couples who took the time to share insights into their marriage. Without you, this would not have been possible. Your openness and caring will always be appreciated.

Third, I would also like to thank my advisors, Dr. Cheryl B. Evans, Chair, Dr. Susan Mosley-Howard and Dr. Glenn Stone. Your professionalism, knowledge, and expertise were greatly appreciated.

I would also like to thank the faculty, staff and graduate students in the Family Studies and Social Work Department for their support and inspiration during the completion of the book, especially, Ms. Lisa Scott, Ms. Tiffany McDowell, PhD, Mrs. Karin Schumacher-Dyke, and Ms. Sara Smith.

Finally, I would like to thank my niece Mrs. Tisha Wimberly Wheeler, the rest of my family for their prayers and support. Special Thanks to Rev. Dr. Harry L. White, Jr. and Dr. Shauntae B. White. Special thanks to Rev. Taijuan O. Fuller for his message "Stay on the Wall for Christ" and to my pastor, Rev. Dr. Frederick A. Wright for his message "Surely Goodness and Mercy…"

CHAPTER 1

Introduction

This book seeks to provide insight from six unique couples sharing information about their married life. The couples articulated the significance and differenences associated with their marital reality. All the individuals, however, indicated that it takes work among other things, to endure long-term marriage successfully. The couples indicated that if by telling their stories, it would make a difference for other couples that are planning to marry, or for couples who are on the journey and at different lifecycles in their marriage, then; it would be worth it. The foundation for this research is to consider long-term African American marriage from a position of strength, encouragement, and appreciation, as opposed to a deficit or pathological model of marriage relationships often portrayed in the media and other venues of African American family life. The authors of "Fighting for Your African American Marriage" discuss the special issues and concerns that confront African American marriages, (for example, protecting children, racism, stereotyped views of black women and men, money, accommodating different backgrounds, attitudes about color, in-laws and kin, the church, etc.) Whitfield, Markman, Stanley, Blumberg, 2001).

Theory

Grounded theory was chosen to study a small sample of African American married couples and the attributes of their long-term marriage success, experiences and relationship in their marital lifecycle.

Grounded theory refers to a theory that is inductive in its approach to qualitative research and it uses a systematic set of procedures to arrive at a theory about a basic social process. (Glaser and Strauss, 1967, and Strauss and Corbin, 1990 as cited by Borgatti.) In this study, the long-term African American marriage is the social process and the grounded theory approach allows the data to develop and emerge from the interviews with the couples directly.

Research in the area of African American marriages reveals that it is extremely difficult to understand African American marriages without being aware of the social, economic, racial, and historical factors that have stressed male female relationships beyond those stresses experienced by majority couples (Pinderhughes, 2002). These societal experiences and the ways African Americans have traditionally responded to them has caused difficulties for marital relationships resulting in a decline of marriages at a rate higher than that of all other racial groups in the U.S. It is further noted by Pinderhuges that the historical perspective of African Americans in the U.S. beginning with their arrival and treatment has influenced all aspects of African American life, especially marriage.

It is important to give voice to African American married couples because limited research has been done to study the experiences of the 43% of black couples who are married. (McKenry & Price, 2000). The authors of this research further state, "…The impact of societal stressors (e.g., racism and discrimination) on black couples' marital relationships, and how black couples establish marital roles and negotiate the

2

completion of marital tasks has historically been neglected. In addition, those factors that predict long-term marriages, and the processes associated with marital transitions and the adjustment of newlywed couples, have been studied less in black couples and other couples of color than in white couples." (McKenry & Price, 2000).

While significant research has been done on the quality of long-term marriages in general, what follows are findings of some studies that are not necessarily of African Americans. These findings will be compared with the research from this study of the African American couples. Reports from a study of couples married between 25 and 46 years reveal a number of essential ingredients for long-term satisfying marriage. The common characteristics emerged despite differences in religion, socioeconomic status, ethnicity, geographic locale, and other demographic variables (Kaslow & Robison, 1996). Researchers from this study were members of the Research Committee of the International Family Therapy Association. The following represents the theoretical concepts of the healthy family and married couples:

Characteristics of Healthy Couples/Families.

1. **Adaptive.** Able to adapt to life cycle changes and to stressful events. Also able to access adequate external resources and use good communication.
2. **Commitment.** Involves recognizing individual's worth and acceptance of the value of the family.
3. **Communication.** Entails clear, open, and frequent communication.
4. **Encouragement.** Ability to instill a sense of belonging while encouraging individual development, an idea encompassed in Stierlin et al.'s (1987) concept of "co-evolution."

3

5. **Appreciation.** The ongoing practice of doing things that are positive for each other, just because with no ulterior motive.
6. **Religion/Spiritual.** Expression of God and going to church or other form of religious expression.
7. **Social.** Connection with the larger society, including extended family, friends, and neighbors, and participation in community/school activities.
8. **Roles.** Flexible role structure and everyone knows and acknowledge their roles and responsibilities which allows for effective functioning as a family during times of crisis and under normal circumstances.
9. **Time.** Sharing both quality and quantity time where family enjoys being together.

Findings from a study of 147 first marriages of over 20 years reported eight characteristics of successful marriages as follows: (Fennell (1987 as cited by Kaslow & Robison 1996);

1. Lifetime commitment to marriage.
2. Respect for one's spouse as a best friend, including mutual self-disclosure.
3. Loyalty to spouse and the expectation of reciprocity.
4. Strong, shared moral values.
5. Commitment to sexual fidelity.
6. Desire to be a good parent.
7. Faith in God and spiritual commitment.
8. Companionship with spouse, including spending a great deal of enjoyable time together over the course of a lifetime.

Findings from a study by Kaslow and Hammerschmidt (1992 as cited by Kaslow & Robison 1996 p. 155) investigated 20 couples married 25- 46 years to elicit ideas as to what made their marriages work well. Their list follows:

1. Trust in each other, which includes fidelity, integrity, and feeling "safe."
2. Good problem solving and coping skills.
3. Permanent commitment to the marriage.
4. Open, honest, good communication.
5. Enjoy spending time together, have fun together, have good senses of humor—yet appreciate some spaces in togetherness for separate activities.
6. Shared value system, interests, and activities.
7. Consideration, mutual appreciation, and reciprocity—easy give and take,
8. Deep and abiding love for one another, enriched by being dear friends and lovers; continue to find one another attractive, appealing, desirable, and interesting.

Couples married for at least 30 years provided their perceptions of the qualities, which sustained their relationship in time of closeness and relational strain. (Robinson, & Blanton, 1993). The characteristics identified by the couples in this study included: intimacy balanced with autonomy, commitment communication, religious orientation, and congruent perceptions of the relationship.

According to Glenn, (1990), as cited by Robison & Blanton, (1993) marital success involves marital stability and marital quality. This means it is not enough to identity success with one dimension of time together, but that the quality of that time together over the duration of marriage as perceived by the couple is important. However, Glenn, as cited by Robison & Blanton, 1993) makes the point that marriages may endure or dissolve regardless of the level of quality, and quality may vary within a marriage. Glenn suggests quality should be considered in conjunction with stability in the study of marital success.

The goals of this study are to consider the account of research in this area in general, but more importantly to highlight the diverse views of African American couples for insight and future research. The primary research questions posed to the couples were:

1. Given the high rates of divorce in general and especially, among African American couples what makes their marriage work, and continue to endure successfully despite the statistics?

2. What are the challenges faced during the marriage lifecycle? For example, challenges associated with being a couple, first time parents, adult children leaving home, becoming grandparents, and retirement, etc. How do couples discuss the processes used to handle conflict and differences? Couples were asked about the level of intimacy throughout the life of their marriage as well.

The significance of this study

The study is important because it adds a dimension to the subject that has not been exhausted in the research literature affirming the lifecycles of African American couples who perceived their marriages as satisfying. It is important to learn about the successful strategies, principles and philosophies these long-term couples have employed over the years. The kinds of things that make for success may be taken for granted, but couples on the journey, may find these concepts helpful if they only had the knowledge of what these couples bring to the table of marriage success. It is anticipated that because of this project future research will be an outcome to further our knowledge base, and further advance program opportunities to facilitate and benefit more African American couples.

CHAPTER 2

Literature Review

Research that examines African American marriages of twenty-five to fifty years or more is limited. However, the literature and research concerning African American marriages and families, as well as other long-term marriages will add historical context, perspective and insight to this study. The literature on this topic of long-term African American marriages, marital lifecycles will provide valuable information and insight to newly married African American couples, as well as couples who may be experiencing similar circumstances at the various marital lifecycles, as the couples who will be interviewed in this study.

While there have been few studies of long-term African American marriages, there have been numerous studies on African American families primarily to try and understand the structure, survival, personal relationships, and status of these families. Many of the studies focused on the dysfunctional characteristics of African American family life. (As cited in Journal of Black Studies, 2000, by Billingsley, 1968, 1992; Gaines, 1997; Hill, 1972; McAdoo, 1992b; Mosley-Howard & Evans, 1995; Staples & Johnson, 1993). It is their view that the historical view of the African American family is seen as a deficit-oriented or deficiency-oriented model and not from a more contemporary view of strength. As cited in Journal of Black Studies, 2000, by Billingsley, 1968, 1992; Gaines, 1997; Hill, 1972; McAdoo, 1992b; Mosley-Howard & Evans, 1995; Staples & Johnson, 1993, they discuss African American families from a family systems theory and Afrocentric worldview as they examine the experiences and status of African American families today. In addition the researchers in that study focused on the cultural aspects of the family such as role flexibility, the extended support systems, and their belief systems. They also examined the structures, roles, strengths, and adaptive characteristics in African American family relationships. As cited in Journal of Black Studies, 2000, by Billingsley, 1968, 1992; Gaines, 1997; Hill, 1972; McAdoo, 1992b; Mosley-Howard & Evans, 1995; Staples & Johnson, 1993, these researchers found in a review of the literature for their study that African American families from the 1960s to the 1990s that family structure was usually examined in terms of marital and parental status with focus on legal and biological connections. The connections influenced the way families problem solved and made decisions and assigned roles. This study pointed out that the positive functions served by marriage and the patterns and connections that go beyond biology and the legal system are rarely examined as strengths in the discussion of African American families. It was noted however "that a study by Hill (1972, 1993) and his associates found that married-couple families are still a strong feature of African American life and that above the poverty level, they constitute a majority of families. Hill noted that married-couple families are much better able to resist the negative pressures of society and take advantage of its opportunities than other types of families." (As cited in Journal of Black Studies, 2000, by Mosley-Howard & Evans, P.428-429).

Pinderhughes, (2002) research concerning African Americans indicated that not until the 1960s have scholars been concerned about the rising divorce rate, decrease in marriage, and the high male/female relationship instability rates among African Americans. As found in a study by Pinsof, (2002), the factors responsible for rising divorce rates in the U.S. and elsewhere are the increased human lifespan, the changes in women's roles, and the shift in values and beliefs about marriage and divorce. The study indicated that divorce among African Americans has been higher than that for other groups—with divorce rates twice that for whites (as cited by Pinderhughes, Tucker & Mitchell-Kerman, 1995). Also, the decline in marriages has been even higher to the point that some experts have expressed fear for the survival of the African American families. In 1960, 78% of African American households included a married couple; this rate decreased to 64% in 1970; and by the late 1980s, only 48% of African American households included both a husband and a wife. The trend reached an all-time low of 39% by 1993 (Billingsley & Morrison-Rodriguez, 1998 as cited by Pinderhughes). According to U.S. Bureau of Census, in 2000, 16% of African American males were married, as compared to 60% of whites; 37% of African American females were married, nearly twice as many unmarried as compared to 57% of white females. The study argues that the contextual conditions and the societal role of African Americans have been responsible for the problems that threaten marital occurrence, quality, and stability. The study also states that limited economic conditions or opportunities, the discrediting of African American identities, and the use of social practices and policies have legitimized inequality (Billingsley& Morrison-Rodriguez, 1988; Lawson & Thompson, 1994 as cited by Pinderhughes).

Further, the significance of slavery, Franklin (1967), Frazier (1966), and Patterson (1998) is cited as the initial factor that sabotaged African American marriages: slaves were forbidden by law to marry in some states, and other states made it difficult for slaves to marry. Any emotional bonds that slaves tried to create were undermined by the beliefs and social structures that viewed African Americans as inferior; males were believed to be oversexed, promiscuous, and incapable of marital commitment; slave sales separated families and disrupted relationships, and females were sexually exploited (Furstenberg, Hershberg, & Modell, 1979; Jordan, 1971; Stamp, 1956 as cited by Pinderhughes). African American males were invisible, except when perceived as aggressive and out of control—a perception that persists today (Boyd-Franklin & Franklin, 1999 as cited by Pinderhughes). Further research indicated that African Americans were not considered to be fully human as reflected in the three fifths compromise in the Constitution which states that, in counting the population, five slaves should be considered equal to three person (Article 1, Section 2, The Constitution of the United States of America as cited by Pinderhughes), and slave fathers of children were not named or listed in birth records. Only the slave mother's name and the name of the mother's owner were recorded. The researcher concluded that this practice... reflects the long-standing tendency in this country to nullify and neglect maleness in African-American families. For all intent and purposes, the African American male was a zero—he did not exist. (Pinderhughes, 1999, p187).

Pinderhughes' research in Nigeria in 1974 among the Yoruba tribes where large number of slaves were captured, confirmed that illegitimacy and one-parent families were patterns that developed after the arrival of slaves in the U. S. The research team found no illegitimacy among the traditional tribe members: if a man impregnated a woman, he married her (Pinderhughes, 1978). Although this custom was facilitated by the practice of polygamy, it also meant that, for those natives being taken from Africa, every mother had a husband and every child had a legal father (Pinderhughes, 1999). Patterson describes the most devastating impact of the "holocaust of slavery" as "the ethnocidal assault on gender roles, especially those of father and husband, leaving deep scars in the relations between Afro-American men and women (1998, p.25 as cited by Pinherhughes).

Landry (2000) discuses the two-parent black and white families in a time when so much emphasis is on the single-parent families, the breakup of families through divorce, and many other ills confronting the contemporary family. Landry conducts a study of "intact" black and white families which remain the norm and the statistical majority among white and, until recently black families as well. The discussion and research are focused on the role of black women as pioneers in changing the traditional family from where spousal roles were well defined and segregated from each other to where spouses, wives, share the breadwinner role, even those wives with small children. Also, one where husbands at least to some degree share in the housework and childrearing responsibilities. The research shows that black and white families played different roles at different times. The data show that black middle-class wives pioneered an egalitarian ideology of the family that contrasted sharply with the domesticity prominent among whites. Black middle-class wives championed a "commitment to family, community and careers which offered a different perspective to womanhood. White women adopted this perspective according to Landry in the 60s and 70s; the civil rights movement influenced them.

Landry also discusses how black families challenged the traditional family paradigm as black wives were exempted from the cult of domesticity and as part of the definition of true womanhood, white society had made it easier for black families to depart from the 19th century paradigm and thus developed alternatives. Again the discussion of African Americans and the impact of slavery and the obstacles to preserving a two-parent family system were discussed. Freedom from the master-slave relationship, they looked forward to their own strategy for survival and for the allocation of family roles.

In the book "Fighting for Your Empty Nest Marriage:

reinventing your relationship when the kids leave home," a survey was conducted of long-term marriages. The research was based on the PREP program (the Prevention and Relationship enhancement Program). Its aims is the to help long-term married couples navigate the issues, conflict, associated with marriage typically discovered after children leave home and the couple are starting what is referred to as the second part of their marriage.

Kinsel, (1983) researched factors related to the relationships of couples married fifty years or more. Although this was a quantitative study, the processes, techniques and instrumentation used will be valuable in this project and study of long-term African American marriages and the family life cycle investigation.

Marriage Cycle 1: Life as a Newly Marriage Couple

Survival tips for African American couples are discussed by Diggs, & Pastor (1998) for example, the importance of extended family and in-laws should not be taken for granted! It is also suggested that investing time in these relationships and supporting a spouse's bonds to his/her own family of origin can reinforce the marital relationship.

Secondly, Diggs, & Pastor stress the value of focusing on the relationship, regardless of income level of either spouse. Furthermore, aspects that contributes to happy marriages such as when husbands who support their wives' decision to work assist with household responsibilities. Moreover, when employed wives are sensitive to their husbands' need for respect and balance of power in the marital relationship is important.

Diggs & Pastor, highlight the importance of building connections to church, neighborhood, and social groups as invaluable resources for friendships that can last for a lifetime, as well as become a buffer and defense for living in a society that still suffers from forms of discrimination. Becoming involved together, as well as having separate interest builds closeness and cooperation in the marriage, as well.

Marriage Cycle 2: Parenting Years

The transition to parenthood has been shown to have an impact on marriages. When couples are in their twenties and become parents for the first time research has shown that these couples are more at risk for marital difficulty and likely divorce. Education levels and marriage expectations are also factors in the quality of the marriage at the time of becoming parents. The manner in which couples negotiate the demands of parenthood will determine the quality and strength of the marriage. (Helms-Erikson, H. 2001.)

Research regarding the type of parenting styles African American parents choose is limited. However, there is considerable research by Baumrind (as cited by Querido, Warner, and Eyberg, 2003 p272) regarding three highly studied parenting styles by mostly European, middle class parents. The three parenting styles defined by Baumrind are authoritarian, authoritative and permissive. Authoritarian parenting is characterized by direct discipline and often physical punishment by one or both parents when children are disobedient or misbehave. The authoritative parenting style is distinguishes parents who provide emotional support, firm limit setting, reasoning and responsiveness to children. The permissive parenting style consists of few demands or restrictions placed on children. There is research that found African American parents are more likely to emphasize shared parenting roles with community members and use of physical punishment more often than European American parents, (Hurd, Moore, & Rogers, 1995 as cited by Querido et al p272.) However the link between physical discipline used by mother's of European descent and that of African-American mothers showed risk factor for disruptive behavior and antisocial behavior for the children of mothers of European descent but did not show the same result for African American families, (McLeod, Kruttschnitt, Dornfield (1994, as cited by Querido et al p. 272.). Positive outcomes for African American children associated with the authoritative parenting style is shown evident for children as young as three years. (Tamis-LeMonda, 1999 as cited by Querido et al, p272.).

A study of working-class Black families reported discipline of young children aimed at obedience, which was not viewed as negative but as caring and appropriate. The intent for emphasizing obedience was a way to demonstrate love and respect as well as to make life easier for the child and to help children achieve in school. (as cited by Peters 1981 in McAdoo, 1997).

Marriage and Raising Adolescents

Interestingly, adolescents who describe their mothers as authoritative report better interpersonal relations than adolescents with authoritarian or permissive mothers. While the debate on what parenting style is most effective, evidence points to the authoritative parenting style as having better outcomes and predicts fewer child behavior problems in young African American children.

Marriage and Launching Young Adult Children (Empty Nesting)

Mackey & O'Brien (1999) completed a study in which a diverse group of couples were interviewed on how their marriage has changed over the years in areas of conflict resolution, sexual relationships, and emotional intimacy. The results from the interview indicated that couples who had launched their children,(also known as empty nesters,) viewed most aspects of their marriage positively except for their sexual relationship. In addition, Mackey & O'Brien found that the couples they interviewed thought conflict was less of a problem in later years of marriage than during the childrearing years. The conflict was more open and direct. Couples appeared to deal with issues in the moment and did not hold back their feelings. In the Mack & O'Brien study it was found that while most aspects of marriage was positive in later years that, however, sexual relationship was found to be less satisfying. What did remain important for the couples who participated in the study was the level of physical contact such as touching without sexual intercourse. This research done by Mackey and O'Brien summarized marriage as a "u shaped" curve where in the beginning of the marriage things are great, but get tough during child rearing years, and after the children leave home their marriage is great again. It appears for some couples that hold on things get better the longer they are married.

In contrast, research has also shown the U-shaped relationship between marital happiness and marital duration not to be necessarily U-shaped. In an analysis based on a fixed-effects pooled time-series model with multiple-wave panel data, findings show declines in marital happiness at all marital durations and no support for an upturn in marital happiness in the later years. The relationship between marital happiness and marital duration is slightly curvilinear, with the steepest declines in marital happiness occurring during the earliest and latest years of marriage. VanLaningham, J., Johnson, D. R., Amato, P. (2001).

Research studies have shown a link between "stress and marriage that focus on a specific aspect of *life* stress and marital quality. For example, a number of studies have focused on stress in and from the workplace and marital quality (Meeks et al., 1986; Jenner, 1988; McLaughlin, Cornier, & Cornier, 1988), while others have focused also on stress and sexuality (Morokoff & Gillilland, 1993) or stress and *life*-stage transitions (Suitor & Pillemer, 1987) and marital quality. Similarly, many of the studies that focus on stress and marital quality in older *marriages* also focus on specific *life* events, like the presence of adult children in the home (Aquilino & Supple, 1991) and the division of household labor in later *life* (Suitor, 1991)." (as cited by Harper, J. M., Schaalie, Bruce, G., Sandberg, J. G. (2000 p2.).

Other studies argue that it is not necessarily the U-shaped

relations that sustains long-term marriages but rather the quality of the marriage relationships is more attributed to the way married persons feel about their marriages and that the marriage is characteristic of the relationship between spouses. (Glen, N. D. (1998).

Marriage and becoming Grandparents:

The study of grandparenthood from the African American perspective has been limited. When studied generally the focus is on the role for grandmothers as a surrogate parent to their grandchildren (Minkler, Roe, and Price, 1992 as cited by Barer, 2001). The surrogate parent role is usually linked to an intervention as a result of substance abuse on the part of the adult children who may produce crack cocaine babies for example (Burton, 1992. as cited by Barer, 2001). Becoming a grandparent for many African Americas is complex and the result difficult circumstances as revealed in research that shows that Black grandparents are more likely to be active participants in the rearing of their grandchildren. (Taylor, R. J., Chatters, L.M., Tucker, M. B., and Lewis, E. (1990.) Studies show that grandmothers are often available for several reasons such as for the adolescent mother, parental illness, and for parents who are incarcerated (Hunter & Taylor, 1998, as cited by Barer, 2001). The media sometimes refers to these grandmothers as the "silent saviors," or "second line of defense."

Because of the changing of our family patterns, grandparents are now taking more active roles in society. For example they are helping raise their grandchildren, in many cases, because of teenage pregnancy, single parenting and divorce (King, 1997.) The research conducted by King, showed that grandparents who have a positive relationship with their grandchildren have had a similar positive relationship with their grandparents when they were young. Those who have not experienced a close-knit bond with their grandparents during childhood do not have a close r relationship with their grandchildren as grandparents.

Geographical distance of grandparent to grandchild can make it difficult to have a close relationship.

Further research related to the importance of the grandparent role indicates that gender of the grandparent is important and that children report to have "warmer, more expressive relationships with grandmothers" (Eisenberg,1988 p205). Women typically are socialized toward maintaining family-based relationships which promotes the strongest ties between grandmothers and granddaughters. However, because male and female roles tend to shift after retirement, some researchers believe there is movement toward unisex gender roles for grandparents in now they relate to grandchildren. Spitz & Ward. (1998). The research by Spitz & Ward suggest that the meaning of grandparenthood an be different for grandmothers and grandfathers. Grandmother typically provide more emotional support to their own children and grandchildren. They may also act as a surrogate parent to grandchildren. Grandfathers are more likely to focus on non-personal issues, such as work or school, and are more likely to offer financial support to grandchildren.

Managing Conflict in the Marriage

Conflict is an accepted aspect of life whenever two or more people or joined together, whether in a family, a corporate board room, or a church business meeting. Conflict will occur in most marriages for certain. The effect of conflict between a married couple and the well-being of their children who experience high marital conflict of their parents has often long-term negative impact. Research shows that children who live in high conflict home environments may experience as many issues as parents who are divorced, or parents who never married. (Burg, J.E. 2003).

"The powerful emotional currents of relationship conflict and the cultural pull to give up on the marriage can overwhelm one's motivation to fight for one's marriage. A strong commitment to the marriage is an invaluable resource in difficult times." (Edwards, 2003, p189). In Fighting for Your African American Marriage, discussions about how couples handle conflict is essential because all couples have problems. The manner in which the couples resolve their problems may differ over the life of the marriage depending on the couple. Although some problems are more difficult then others, couples who seem to manage use a common set of skills and attitudes such as working as a team, not rushing to a solution, but taking time to understand the issues together (Whitfield, Markman, Stanley, Blumberg, 2001).

Factors to consider in Long-term marriage success

There are likely as many factors that account for the success of long-term marriages as there are for each marriage. One author reveals the power of relationships that endure through extreme hardship. A study of couples who have survived despite the alcoholism of one partner was examined. (Shirely, 2002). The couples in the study revealed the resources and strengths available to them which helped them endure in a complex relationship. The author dealt with the concept and framework of family resiliency in an unique an compelling manner based on the marital relationship rather than individual experience. Shirley discusses couple's who were interviewed accounts of courage, commitment, and romantic love, as well as resentment, frustration, and difficulty in communication, so as to provide insight into what helps some marriages succeed in the face of considerable obstacles.

In an article that discusses the dilemmas facing Christian marriages, a lack of commitment is said to be the single biggest threat to the institution of marriage. Anything that undermines commitment to marriage as a Divine institution, designed by God to last for a lifetime, is a threat to the institution of marriage." (Edwards, 2003). Cohabitation and an increase in casual attitude toward intimate relationship and commitment among young singles today is described as seeking "relationships without rings, sex without strings." (Popenoe & Whitehead, 2001, as cited by Edwards 2003.)

Edwards further states his belief that a society with a pleasure-oriented, individualism; materialism and programs in the media seeks to destroy the value system of commitment to long-term marriage. Edwards believes that the sexual exploitation of our youth has profound undermining impact on the institution of marriage. In addition, Edwards believes partner's lasting commitment to the relationship is the essential attitude that underlines each partner's motivation to invest in the relationship, willingness to give the relationship a high priority in one's life, and perseverance in working out problems inevitable in intimate relationships.

It is noted that in the Christian community that the divorce rate among Evangelical Christians is about the same as other groups. Barna Research Group reported that the divorce rates for Evangelicals, Born-Again Christians, and other groups were all around 34% (Barna, 2001 as cited by Edwards 2003 p. 1992.) Edwards suggests that a mentoring program for churches in order to support marriages. The program consists of older experienced couples who meet regularly with younger couples to encourage and help with understanding reality including the joy and struggles of maintaining a life-long marriage relationship.

Although the divorce rates for couples with religious beliefs and practices are relatively the same as in the secular community, African Americans find emotional, spiritual, and intellectual support and satisfaction at church. Reaching out to others is a related strength of African Americans; getting involved in a church group provides the opportunity to both give and receive social support. Social support is crucial for marital well-being, (Olson, D. H., & DeFrain, J.,1994).

Maintaining Intimacy in the marriage

Factors of attribution for happiness and good communication

in marriage were found in emotionally healthy wives who communicate more and tend to be noncomplaining; and in emotionally healthy husbands who tend to play down problems and communicate well with their wives. (Houck & Daniel, 1994.) Most would agree that intimacy is a key element of marital quality.

Summary of the Literature Review

While the literature related to long-term marriages provides perspectives based on qualitative, quantitative and some longitudinal studies over the course of many lifetimes (in an attempt to reveal what makes for marital success whether for African Americans or other ethnicity) there still remains a need for further insight. This study attempts to bring additional insight through the stories of a small sample of African American couples.

CHAPTER 3

Methodology

Assumptions and Rationale for a Qualitative Design

A key assumption of a qualitative study is interest in interpretation of meaning from how people make sense of their lives, and experiences as well as how they relate these realities in the organization of the world. As a qualitative researcher this writer is interested in the richness and meaning that long-term African American married couples give to their lives as a married couple. This exploratory qualitative study was designed to gain this information by personally interviewing six African American couples who have been married for twenty-five years, or more.

Type of Design Used

Grounded theory was chosen to study a small sample of African American married couples and the attributes of their long-term marriage success, experiences and relationship in their marital lifecycle.

Grounded theory refers to a theory that is inductive in its approach to qualitative research and it uses a systematic set of procedures to arrive at a theory about basic social processes. (Glaser and Strauss, 1967, and Strauss and Corbin, 1990 as cited by Borgatti,) There are three basic elements to grounded theory, concepts, categories, and propositions. (Corbin and Strauss (1990, p.7). Strauss and Corbin (1998) state,

The first step is describing, which is depicting, telling a story, sometimes a very graphic detailed one, without stepping back to interpret or explain why certain events occurred and not others. The second step is conceptual ordering, which is classifying events and objects along various explicitly stated dimensions, without necessarily relating the classifications to each other to form an overarching explanatory scheme. The last step is theorizing, which is the act of constructing from data an explanatory scheme that systematically integrates various concepts through statements of relationship. (p.25).

Once a valid theory has been developed it will enable the research to explain and predict events, thereby providing guides to action (Strauss & Corbin, 1998).

In this study, long-term African American marriage is the social process, and the grounded theory approach allows the data to develop and emerge from the interviews with the couples directly. Face-to-face interview approach was used to gain knowledge of the salient principles and characteristics that enable these couples to have enduring marriages across the marital lifecycle in their own voices given no two marriages are alike. This study strives to provide an in-depth and authentic view of how some African American marriages thrive through opportunity and through challenging experiences.

The primary research questions posed to the couples were:

1. Given the high rates of divorce in general and especially, among African American couples what makes your marriage work, and continue to endure successfully despite the statistics?
2. What are the challenges faced during the marriage lifecycles?

PARTICIPANTS

A non-probability sample of six married African American couples was created primarily through recruitment of African American churches, personal contacts, and referrals by faculty, and graduate students in the family studies department of a Midwestern university and surrounding city. Participants ranged in age from 52 to 72 years of age.

The mean for number of years married was 40.8 years, with a range of 33-50 years of marriage. The mean age at time of marriage for husbands was 22.8, with a range of 21-24 years of age. Wives' mean age at time of marriage was 19.5, with a range from 17-20 years of age.

The education levels for individuals in this sample were varied. All except three, two wives and one husband, graduated from high school, one wife attended vocational school, one wife attended college, one wife had graduated from college, one wife had a post graduate degree, one husband had attended college, two husbands completed at least an undergraduate degree and two husbands had completed a post graduate degree.

All couples who shared income had an income of at least $20,000; four couples had an income of at least 50,000. One couple did not share income information.

Almost all subjects were affiliated to some extent with a specific religious denomination.

All couples had at least one child. The number of children ranged from two – eight. Two couples had at least one adult child living at home. One couple had a child and a grandchild living with them.

Three couples were retired, of three couples one wife was retired, the husband worked outside the home full-time, and one couple had both the husband and the wife working full-time

INSTRUMENT:

Unstructured interviews were conducted with husbands and wives together in their home. Couples were encouraged to be open and discuss freely. There were six interview questions to guide participant discussion for telling their stories of the marital lifecycles from their personal perspective. As the couples began answering the guided questions, additional probing questions were used to explore the area in more detail.

The interviews averaged an hour in length and were audiotape-recorded. They were transcribed and coded into analytic memos for each individual and for each of the couples by the interviewer. The memos summarized the salient views raised by the couples.

CHAPTER 4

Findings

The purpose of this study was to examine the marital lifecycle experiences of African American couples to ascertain those strategies, which allow these couples to endure in times of challenge and adversity as well as in times of joy and happiness. A grounded theory approach was taken to have the data emerge directly from the participant's experiences through the marital lifecycle, as opposed to developing a hypothesis before hand. Husbands and wives responded to open-ended interview questions, which permitted uninterrupted responses in their own words. However, this researcher did probe responses to some questions for clarity or for further explanation to a question, periodically. Several themes were discovered with the application of this method.

Data Analysis

Analysis of the data suggested the following six key elements were associated with the successful journey of their long-term marital lifecycles: communication, intimacy, commitment, parental role models, religion/spirituality, and education. In addition, the marital lifecycles analyzed consisted of life as a couple, married with children, work/careers, empty nest years and retirement.

CHAPTER 5

The Couples

Themes for Marital Success: (Note: names changed to protect privacy)

Sam and Sadie. Sam is 71 years old and married at age 24, Sadie is 66 years old and married at age 19. They have been married for 47 years and have two adult children and six grandchildren. Sam is retired after working 41 years at a company. The Sadie was retired after 30 years but she recently returned to work after her husband recovered from a serious health issue. Both are actively involved in church and their spirituality. This couple mentioned five of the six themes (communication, intimacy, commitment, parental role models, and religion/spirituality.) Sam began the interview with an opening comment about his beliefs for a good marriage: *"If you love each other, the marriage should last. There are five things you can go by having a good marriage: caring, commitment, togetherness, you have to be together, trust each other and romance."* Sam indicated he was attracted to his wife when he first saw her. However, the wife indicated, *"It was not love at first sight, but that he was driving a very pretty car."* This couple emphasized communication as key to making the marriage work. The wife expressed that they agreed to "never go to bed angry." They both conveyed the importance of church life in their marriage. The wife said "the main thing is that our parents were in church and kept us in Sunday school, I *said "when I get grown I ain't never going to Sunday school."* Being in church and being a Christian plays a big part in marriage. The husband indicated he had been active in church since the age of 10. They both credit having parents as good role models for having a good marriage. However, the Sadie who was raised primarily by her mother and stepfather indicated that prior to her mother's remarriage she had lived in an abusive family environment as a young child had and it had an impact on her. She was determined when she did marry to make it a good marriage. Sam earned the respect of his Sadie's parents early on by showing respect for their daughter. This couple saw communication and handling conflict or arguments in the proper way as essential. For example, Sam said *"it takes two to argue, when you start to argue, one needs to be quite and listen."* As intimacy was one of the themes that most couples discussed, this couple expressed that holding hands and kissing was important as well as saying the words "I love you," and giving cards, flowers and gifts on special occasions was important.

John and Martha. John is 58 years old and married at age 23, Martha is 55 years old and married at age 19. They have been married for 36 years and have two adult children, (one is deceased.) They have eight grandchildren. John retired after working 32 years at a company, but is currently working part-time. Martha is and has always been a homemaker. This couple, also, connected with five of the six themes: communication, commitment, church/spirituality, intimacy, and parental role model. This wife indicates that in the beginning, they *"never go to bed angry"* and that works for her because she came from a broken home and commitment is very important to her. Furthermore, this wife *said "I think everybody goes into a marriage with the intent of doing what's right but sometime you know if you* *don't communicate, if you don't have an understanding of differences you can get yourself in trouble. You have to sit down and discuss things.*" John says that they had some arguments and he won't deny that, but we never hit, or nothing like that—"*there was never any physical abuse.*" Martha talks about the issue of physical abuse and she states that *abuse is not going to help the matter at all. Actually, it makes things worse and it's not going to help a child because you're teaching them physical abuse.* She said, "we don't fight, but I might argue with you all day." John points out that in his bringing up that his father never hit my mother either; he was really strict about that with the boys. He has seven brothers and one sister, and his father didn't tolerate physical abuse. He takes pride in knowing that many of his family and friends say he is like his father. In addition, his mother was a stay-at-home mom and his father provided for them and he figure that's what I am supposed to do, that is how he was raised. Conversely, Martha comes from a broken family and the two of them bonded around the issue of her staying at home while he worked. Intimacy was important to this couple as well. Martha expressed that she and her husband share life, as one and that they are very close. However, she sometimes teases her husband and says that he takes her for granted, because he is not an affectionate person. Affection to her means she would like a Valentine Day card, or better than anything, hearing "I appreciate you or I love you." John says that "I do say I love you, well I don't say it all the time, sometime I might say in a joking way. He says he is always touching and hugging her and she tries to get away from me." He admits that "maybe I should say it (I love you) more because his goal is to be married 50 years. My father and mother had 50 plus years of marriage."

Phillip and Deborah Phillip is 54 years old and married at age 21, Deborah is 55 years old and married at age 22. They have been married for 33 years and have two adult children. They have one grandchild. Phillip is a semi-retired engineer and the Deborah is a retired educator. This couple connected to three of six themes: intimacy, communication, education, and commitment. They met in high school, and they were committed to their education and to each other. They attended college in different locations and communicated long distance for several years. They were married two months after Deborah's college graduation. Phillip had dropped out after his sophomore year from a college in northern Ohio because of what he believed was racism. He was in a freshman class of the first blacks ever to live on campus and there were some racial incidents. He enlisted in the military and he and his Deborah would communicate with each other by sending cassette tapes to each other, writing letters, and telephone calls. This was during the Vietnam War era. The personal computer technology and e-mail was not available during that time. Phillip completed his college degree after his honorable discharge from the military. As for intimacy in the marriage, the couple expressed having a really good and wonderful sex life for most of the marriage, but have experienced some diminished activity level which they both attribute to lack of privacy because of adult children returning home, and the presence of a grandchild living in the home, as well as other stresses, both physical and emotional. Phillip expressed concern that things may not get back to where they were, *"sex is important and I don't want to loose it."* This couple associated the lack of good parental role models for a good marriage as a factor in their being determined to make their marriage successful. They were willing to doing whatever it takes. Phillip explained that even as a teenager he knew he *"wanted to be married and have children of his own because he grew up without a father.* However, he did have a relationship with his father but his parents were never married, he said, *"I went through some difficult times being raised by a single mother."* In addition, Phillip wanted to be the kind of parent his mother and father never could be given their situation. So when he met Deborah , they fell in love, he saw her as a good person, and he saw her as a good mate; they have become soul mates, as well that what's kept their relationship together through all the stuff, a tremendous love and a tremendous respect for her. Deborah says the same thing applies to her as far as what she wanted in life. However, she came from a nuclear family and her parents were married for more than 50 years, but they have not been in a happy marriage according to her; she feels that her mother regrets some of the choices she has made with regard to marriage.

Joe and Ruth. Joe is 68 years old and married at age 23, Ruth is 65 years old and married at age 20. They have been married for 45 years and have two adult children. They do not have grandchildren. Joe is an educator, and Ruth is currently retired and a homemaker. This couple connected with four of the six themes: parental role models, communication, intimacy and education. This couple married only four months after they met. The husband said they had plenty of time to get to know each other after the fact. What helped their marriage be successful from Ruth's point of view was her Joe's patience. For example, Ruth thought that she needed a lot of work because she made many unreasonable demands when they were first married, but her husband was very patient with her. She said she lacked trust in men because of having come from a broken home. Joe said he was able to be patient because his parents had a long-term marriage and his father was his role model. His father had his mom on a pedestal and got her whatever… he did his best to try to please her and kind of …said that's what men were suppose to do. His father never missed a holiday where he didn't give his mother something; she always had nice things and he thought she should be taken care of. His parents were married for 43 years until his mother's death. His grandparents also had a long-term marriage of over 65 years.

Joe expressed that he and Ruth discovered that 50/50 doesn't work; most marriages are 90/10, sometimes it flip-flops and takes turn. It's not evenly balanced, so sometimes you give a lot more, and sometimes you get a lot more and I don't know how we came to that, we just kind of did it. Ruth conveyed a time when communication was important for their future in that her husband decided to go to college and work full-time which meant that they would spend very little time together. She said what made it work was that they discussed it, he said it's not going to be easy, it was going to be tough and he wasn't sure that she would be able to deal with it, so she said *"I guarantee you I can last as long as you do."* She was willing to make the sacrifice for a better future for their family. As for their level of intimacy in the marriage, Joe expressed that he always thought intimacy important and it's very satisfying in their relationship. Ruth expressed that the husband is more touchy feely than she is and she thinks that is because of her background having come from a broken home and the lack of affection shown in her home. She is happy with their level of intimacy. This couple also expressed the importance of having good relationships with their in-laws was key to a good marriage.

Ben and Ellen. Ben is 73 years old and married at age 23, Ellen is 67 years old and married at age 17. They have been married for 50 years and have eight adult children. They have 25 grandchildren and 10 great grandchildren. Ben is a retired jet engine builder, and Elise is a homemaker. The couple mentioned four of the seven themes: communication, parental role models, religion, and intimacy. For example, Ben indicates that honest communication, being fair, loving and spending time together are all important in making their marriage work. Both Ben and Ellen stressed the importance of having strong supportive parents and grandparents who taught them and discussed how to be a good husband and wife. Ben said the training that his parents gave him, for example, his father would say, *"Son treat your wife right, now, don't be fighting her don't be jumping on her, you treat her right now."* He said this training stayed with him. Ellen said her grandfather who raised her was a good role model and teacher. For example he taught don't let the sun go down on your wrath, so if you argue, don't go to bed angry. Ellen said it is important to understand each others likes and dislikes. Religion plays a major part in this couples life. Ellen says they tried to live according to the teachings of the Bible even when they were not in church. For example, they would have family prayer at home when unable to attend church.

Ken & Tisha. Ken is 57 years old and married at age 23, Tisha is 54 years old and married at age 20. They have been married for 34 years and have two adult children. Ken is currently working as a law enforcement officer and Tisha is an educator. This couple mentioned three of the six themes: education, religion and intimacy. Tisha communicates that what makes their marriage work is that they give each other space, meaning she and her husband do a lot of things that they really want to do, and they do not have to do things together. They are involved in different activities; for example, she travels extensively alone or with other family members for work, or vacations. Ken said mutual respect, devotion, taking responsibility and his wife being very organized is what helps their marriage succeed. This couple met in college and Tisha was able to complete her degree after they were married, while her husband had been drafted into the military during the Vietnam War. He completed his degree after being honorably discharged from the military. Both Ken and Tisha indicate religious affiliation, however, Tisha attends church regularly and Ken does not attend church on a regular basis.

Marital Lifecycles

For purpose of this research, the marital lifecycles identified and discussed in the interviews with the six couples were: <u>Married Couple</u>, <u>married with children and parenting</u>, <u>work/careers</u>, <u>empty nest</u>, and <u>retirement years</u>. The findings from this part of the interviews was quite revealing in terms of time of challenge, joy and happiness as described in the interviews.

Sam and Sadie

As a couple. Sam and Sadie communicated that the first four years of marriage were lovely. They lived in a one-room apartment, but it was the best of times. They had to share a bathroom with the neighbors during this time and were quite happy when they were able to move to a three-room apartment. They both were establishing their careers and building seniority at their jobs. Sadie also attended vocational college during this time and took advantage of her employer's tuition reimbursement plan. This time of being married and childfree allowed Sadie to advance quickly in her vocation as an electroencephalogram technician. They had agreed to get pregnant after five years of marriage.

Married with children. Sam and Sadie were very happy with the birth of their first child. Sadie indicated it was so much fun and that everybody wanted to help and give advice. She had a supportive network of extended family and friends to help in the beginning as she did return to work soon after the birth. Their second child was born six years later and the birth was difficult where both the mother and child were in serious condition. Sadie and her husband decided not to have any more children as a result. Sam communicated, "I was proud of myself," after becoming a father.

During the childrearing years, Sadie found childcare to be an issue early-on and made arrangements with her employer to change her work hours to night shift so that she and Sam could provide the childcare. Sadie said when her husband Sam came in from work, *"she was ready to go out the door; she had everything ready, food cooked, house cleaned."* Sam said, *"she would go to work and I would take care of the baby."* When asked how he felt about that, Sam said *"I feel all right, I take care of my kids, I rather take care of them myself because you don't know how other people are going to take care of your kids."* Sam and Sadie were very involved in school activities with their children. Sadie and said that her husband Sam would always go to the school and the teachers and students all loved him. They would work with the school system, the teachers, and PTA involvement as well. The Sam said that when their children were adolescents they, as parents were always in control. They talked with their children and today have a very close relationship with them, as well as with the grandchildren.

Empty Nest. Sam and Sadie experienced their first major challenge in their marriage when the Sam became ill with cancer. Sadie said it was very stressful. Sadie retired early to provide care giving for her husband Sam. After recovery, they both enjoy spending time together, and working with their hobbies and family business.

John and Martha

As couple. Martha communicated that for her the first five years were the roughest because they have a lot to get use to and learn about their two personalities. John and Martha started their marriage with one child. John said it was unique because when they first married he had a family, a wife and a son so they were never alone. Martha indicated having responsibility for a child while getting use to each other took some adjustment. She basically raised their son as a single parent early-on. Martha said *"he was away all those years, so as a single parent for four years still have to get adjusted...I think everybody goes into a marriage with the intent of doing what's right but, if you don't communicate and you don't have an understanding of differences you can get yourself in trouble.*" Prior to their marriage the John was in the military and in the Vietnam War and he said, "*I went to Vietnam…and communicated back and forth with her and really didn't think that I would be home because the area that I was in was pretty rough, and I was fortunate to come back home and she was waiting for me.*" So, they were married soon after his return from the military.

Married with children. John and Martha had two children, but **they also served as surrogate parents to two nephews over the course of their marriage**. John shared that they always had someone. The nephews were treated the same as their children. When asked about the additional family responsibilities and the impact on their marriage, the Martha indicated she didn't think it had any negative impact. In fact she thought it made her son happy to have other boys in the home to play with. John said as far as food and other necessities he provided what was needed. Martha expressed that their nephews look to her husband as a father figure.

John and Martha **experienced several challenges and personal crises during the parenting years.** First, one nephew whom they had helped raise, but had returned to his parents as a young adult, had died through violence, he had been shot and killed. One year later, their son had died in a diabetic coma at the age of 28 years old. Soon after that Martha's lost her grandfather who had raised her, and the John lost his mother. Martha said that the nineties were very bad years for them. In addition, as it relates to parenting, John and Martha faced difficulty with their adolescent daughter who had been diagnosed with a serious illness. Martha indicates that her husband, John was overly protective of their daughter, but they faced the difficulty together. **This diagnosis put a financial strain on the family as well.**

This couple spent some time in the grieving process, to the point where they both drifted away from the church and from each other. For example John commented, "*When I was hit with all this, I wasn't as good as Job was. I just couldn't take it." Martha indicated that they were both grieving in their own way.*

Grandparenting. John and Martha have eight grandchildren and the Martha says that John has a special love and affection for all the grandchildren. John says he loves spending time wit the grandchildren. He revealed that, *"I just thought about this a few minutes ago, maybe I didn't spend quite enough time with my kids so I think I am mostly making up for it with the grandkids. When the kids were coming up, when I got married I had a child and I always worked but I love these grandchildren. They all get on my lap."*

Work/Career. John is the breadwinner in this family. **During the early times of their marriage he shares that it was kind of rough, because he was fresh on the job and wasn't making a lot of money. He had taken an entry level position and it took time to earn seniority.** He had saved some money while in the service to help with the finances because it was important to stretch the money. **Martha never worked outside the home and she expressed that her husband handles the money and does a good job of it, even though they may disagree about some things.** Martha also shared that she never was interested in a career after she was married. She always felt that her child should have a two-parent family, because she didn't have one. However, **Martha felt that her role was that of nurturer and she was very protective of her husband and the children.** Because her husband John often worked overtime hours and took part-time jobs occasionally, she contributed by taking care of everything at home. **For example, she did all the housework, inside and outside. She shoveled snow, cut the grass and did the interior painting on a regular basis. She enjoyed it and felt that was her way of contributing to the family and protecting her husband.** In addition, Martha said, *"when there was a snow emergency, I would get up and fix his lunch, and breakfast, no matter what time* *of day or night...I took care of him, and some people use to ask why do you get up? I felt that was what I was suppose to do, I could go back to bed."* She indicated while she felt obligated, but at the same time she wanted to do those things. **Martha expressed that she thinks her role in the family helped their marriage be successful.** John confirmed that his wife did all those things, and that she is the "glue" that keeps them together. **John said that Martha was looking out for him and he appreciates her for it.**

Philip and Deborah

As couple. Philip and Deborah were married soon after Deborah had graduated from college in the month of July and were separated the next month, in August, three weeks later because Philip was in the military service. Deborah lived near her parents and worked as an educator while her husband, Philip was away in the military. She remembers him calling her one Christmas from France. When he returned to the States he would try to visit her as often as possible. They had bought a car just so he could drive several hundred miles, ten hours, to visit his wife when he had time off and on most weekends. Phillip was in a serious car accident on one of his trips home when he said, *"I woke up off interstate in the middle of the median and had no recollection of how I got there and what woke me up was the State trooper beating on the window of the car."* Deborah explained that that weekend, they decided after school was out and she had finished teaching for the term, she would move to where he was stationed. So the day after school was out they move. She was excited because **this would be the first time they were going to be together as a married couple and that was after two years**. The Philip revealed that *"those were the best three years of our life, we lived in military housing.* We didn't have nothing, but we had each other, we had friends, the military did provide a lot of things, you could go to the movie for 25 cents. It was the 70's and you're talking about first run movies, we used to eat at the restaurants on the base for five dollars or something like that. We had the beach, just a lot of nice stuff..."

Married with children. Their first child was born while they were still in the military; After being honorably discharged from the military, they came back home, and the Philip went back to school. He communicated, " Oh **I always wanted to go back to school, because I had two years in college toward an engineering degree**. I said I have a family I have to take care of and I need to find a program that will keep me in the field..."

This couple was challenged during the parenting years when their son was diagnosed with a serious illness at five years old. **The couple sought family counseling in order to deal with the issues their son was facing**. The issues challenged their marriage and they both expressed that counseling helped the marriage and the family. The couple have two adult children and one grandchild and they have always been very involved and supportive parents. Their children are both college graduates and they are very proud of them.

Empty Nest. Philip and Deborah encountered several challenges after they both had retired early and were looking forward to a different and exciting lifestyle for the two of them, now that their adult children were out on their own. Philip conveyed that both adult children had moved back home for various reasons and he and his wife wanted to be supportive while they worked some of their issues out. This was a time of challenge and personal stress for the couple as these changes in living arrangements put added unanticipated financial burden on the household. At the same time, the Deborah's parents became ill and she had the additional responsibility of caring for both parents for a while.

Work/Career. As a result of the dynamics in the family, Philip chose to go back to work to relieve some of the financial burden. Deborah also chose to accept part-time work in education but before she could get started she found herself providing childcare for her live in grandchild. Although she and her husband have a wonderful relationship with their grandchild there is strain because of different childcare expectations the mother (daughter) has. Philip communicated that they have come to realized that they cannot expect their children to raise the grandchildren exactly as they did and they need to respect different parenting styles to some degree. *Philip discussed the importance of counseling for the family, "Men don't seek counseling because it is perceived as a sign of weakness. The times we had, the most problem with our relationship were those times when we didn't talk. You have to be willing to sit down and talk with your wife no matter how difficult you may think; we're not perfect because there are still things...*

Joe and Ruth

As a couple. This couple met and married four months after meeting. Joe thought his wife was cute and that they were compatible with common interest. Ruth expressed that they did not have a lot of dates because he worked a lot, but he proposed marriage in a round about way, by asking her to leave the state with him. He actually meant that they should get married first. He had a car and Ruth thought that was important.

Married with children. Ruth indicated that when she became pregnant she had done a great thing in the family because she had the first son in the family since her husband was born. Ruth conveyed that she has a good relationship with her adult son. Joe indicated that parenting their son had it's challenges. Because the couple moved around some when their son was pre-teen and teenage and they think that may have impacted the son's inappropriate behavior. For example, the parents learned that their son was being truant from school at a time when he was two credits from graduating from high school. The son was always a good student, and always had done very well until late in his senior year of high school.

He did with extra help graduate from high school. **Another parenting challenge for the couple was that their son had gotten into some drug use and other inappropriate behavior.** The couple sought family counseling and communicated **that this adversity strengthen their marriage.** Their second child a daughter, presented a series of parenting challenges as well. For example, during Ruth's pregnancy it was found that she had an atopic pregnancy in the fallopian tubes, the baby was never in the womb, so she free floated and it wasn't realized until time to deliver. The doctors were quite surprised to find the baby behind the uterus. This was a real crisis as she, almost bled to death. Joe always perceived his daughter as very needy and he attributes this to her not being sheltered by the womb. Ruth felt that the baby was ok since she had a good weight at birth, over seven pounds. The mother daughter bonding was not there and it is still a difficult relationship. Ruth feels her daughter and husband have a better relationship. Joe revealed that there were real challenges with their daughter when she reached late adolescent. For example, **their daughter quit high school and ran off to get married.** He and his wife did not know where she was for quite sometime. The daughter eventually contacted her mother's best friend and communicated where she was and that she had gotten married. Joe and Ruth later learned that their son-in-law had been arrested for drug use and that he had been real abusive to their daughter. This father believes there was a poor self-esteem issue, which is incomprehensible to him. Joe and Ruth do not have grandchildren, but they have been providing childcare for a nephew since the baby was about six weeks old, he is now two years old.

Work/Career. Joe was the breadwinner for about the first fifteen years of the marriage. There were periods of time when Ruth would work only a little and later after about four or five years she worked fulltime in a career. Joe began to perceive his wife differently than when they were first married. For example,

"She was no longer his other half, a helpmate...and she said to him one day when I suggested that I wanted her to go somewhere with me, she said I have to go to work and she said to me you have to understand that my job is as important to me as your job is important to you..." Joe communicated that he was somewhat taken back because he had old time views and was just doing what he thought he was suppose to do. **Joe indicated he had some growing to do in terms of letting go and understanding the notion of equal status and sharing responsibility.** Ruth indicated that her mother taught her to be independent, didn't matter if you're married, or not whatever, you still need to be independent, you need to be able to take care of yourself. It took her a little longer but she finally went to work full-time. She felt that she needed to establish herself as an independent person, because, if her husband was not there, she would have to do so. **She did not want to be in a situation where he was gone and then have to figure it out.** She also enjoyed having her own money and not relying on her husband for money for the things she wanted. Joe indicated that they always had our money and her money and they generally lived on his salary for most of the household necessities.

Ben and Ellen

As a couple. Ben and Ellen met the day before Ben left to join the military. Upon his return from basic training, they dated and were soon married. Ellen communicated that Ben had earned the respect of her mother and father and because he was being very nice he had won her over, too.

Married with children. Ben and Ellen became parents one year after they were married and had a total of eight children. Ellen felt that being a parent was wonderful even though she didn't know what to expect at first from a baby. For example, on the first day home with the baby she laid her down on the bed and went to another room for a moment and came back and the baby was not on the bed. The baby had rolled behind the bed and fortunately was not injured. Ben communicated that Ellen was the sergeant of childrearing. He was very happy with his girls but when the fifth child was a boy he was very proud of having a boy child. Ben recalled that when dealing with teenagers and they said they were going to be at a particular place his wife would insist on their being where they should be and if not she would get in the car and go looking for them and find out what was going on in their lives. **They used prayer a lot to reinforce their parenting styles as well as the teaching from their parents.** For example, Ellen indicated they never let a New Year come in without the family being on their knees for prayer. In addition **Ellen used some parenting techniques she learned from her grandfather such as, when one child had a tendency to get loud and have an attitude, she would get the Bible and tell the child the Bible says a soft voice turns away wrath, a harsh voice stirs the wrath.** She said "when you talk to me like that I want to get a switch, so you talk to me right," and that worked. **Another technique she used was to get a piece of paper and write a scripture on it and stick it up in the bathroom and the child would realize they were doing wrong when they read it.** One of their children used this approach with her children and because she has a computer, she is able to make beautiful scripture signs and she puts them on the wall for her children. **They always demanded that the children finish high school and several of their children attended college.** Ben and Ellen have very good relationships with their children, grandchildren and great grandchildren. Two of their grandsons play professional football and they are very proud of that. The couple have experienced some challenges as parents, for example, **one of their daughters became involved with a guy who was involved in drugs, and strung out; they were married with two children**. Their son-in-law had been in and out of jail and had tried to get his life together by attending church regularly. Unfortunately, he eventually ended up getting killed. The wife communicated that whenever any of her children would call with a serious problem, no matter the time of day or night she and her husband would respond and try to help. Ellen's parents always encouraged and told her not to put the kids out, she said let them come back home. She would rather have her children and grandchildren at home with them instead of in the streets.

Work/Career. Ben was the primary breadwinner and indicated that he tried to be a good provider, for example he said *" I would bring my money home and give it to her, because I knew she knew how to take care of it; she knew how to stretch a dollar."* Ellen communicated that her grandfather taught her to save; he would tell her *"if you make a dollar, save a dime."* Ellen indicated that if the money was a little short she would offer to take a job for a while and Ben was ok with that as long as the children were taken care of. They relied on the extended family for childcare for the times that she was employed outside the home Ben would provide some childcare if he was not working.

Empty Nest. Ben and Ellen have two adult children living with them, temporarily. Ellen expressed that they did look forward to the thought that they now have problems solved and all the big stuff is out of the way and they can do what they want to do now, but that lasted only about a year. However the two of them get away on vacations more.

Retirement. Ben has been retired since 1993 and he spends his time doing house remodeling and gardening. Ellen considers herself retired because she is not currently working outside the home.

Ken and Tisha

As a couple. Ken and Tisha met in college and dated about two years, prior to the Ken getting drafted into the military and being stationed in Germany for sometime. He came home on leave and they were married and he had to leave again. Tisha was a junior in college and stayed and graduated and then she taught school while her husband, Ken was in Vietnam.

Married with children. Ken indicated that this was a challenging time for them because he was not sure where they would end up living. Tisha indicated their first child was born before they were married and that they got married right after the baby was born. They were newly married, had a baby, while she was still in college and her husband was in Germany and then in Vietnam. Ken indicated he was gone for a good two years before they actually became a couple. Tisha was mom and dad, and a student for sometime. **They had the help of their parents for childcare while Tisha was finishing school.** Ken's parents cared for the baby at first and then Tisha's parent's provided childcare; this childcare arrangement was a big help. The child was three years old when the family relocated. **The couple have two adult children and they both expressed that raising them required an investment of time and resources to make sure they had what they needed.** They spent a lot of quality time with the children. Ken indicated that his wife, Tisha handled the primary childcare early on as he was on-call for his career a lot. He also communicated that they tried to do as much as possible together as a family, such as travel. Tisha conveyed that both the children were involved in many different things; for example, one daughter played the viola and was in the international orchestra. **She shared that her husband, Ken would drive their daughter for two years straight once a month out of town, about a four-hour drive to rehearse.** Also, the daughter spent six weeks in Europe before graduating from high school, and another daughter also involved in music played the cello and was involved in the youth symphony as well as played soccer for many years. Both of their daughters are college graduates. Tisha expressed that **she is particularly happy about one daughter receiving** her doctorate degree because she had been diagnosed with a serious illness at the beginning and it was a struggle, but she was able to complete her degree in dentistry. In addition, one daughter is a Captain in the military serving currently in Iraq. Ken indicated that they invested a lot in their children but it paid off, and having two beautiful daughters would be one of the highlights of their marriage. They are looking forward to the birth of their first grandchild later this year.

Work /career. Both Ken and Tisha are currently working. Ken indicates he would like to be retired, but he has about seven more years to work before becoming retirement eligible. He works in the area of law enforcement and expressed that he really hates what he does for his career. The nature of the work is stressful and he tries not to talk about the details or bring home some of the issues he deals with on a daily basis, for example, he encounters people who are HIV-positive. Tisha communicated that she thinks her husband is overly concerned about certain things and that she does not feel impacted negatively by his career issues.

Tisha who is currently working as an educator and although she is retirement eligible expressed that retirement plans are unclear and that is why she is still teaching.

Empty Nest. Ken and Tisha have been challenged by a major illness as Tisha has been a breast cancer survival for two years. Tisha expressed that she was particularly *"challenged by the news of the cancer because she thought she had done everything she could possible do to stay healthy. She said there was no family history of cancer and she was angry. It was a challenge for all of them and it still is a challenge. They dealt with it the best they could."* One daughter came home on leave from the military to spend time with her while she was having chemo, and the other daughter came also to provide support. Ken communicated that *"at the time I was upset and thinking the worst could happen and hoping the worst did not happen and just tried to be as sensitive as possible, trying not to upset her. It was the first major illness the family experienced."*

CHAPTER 6

Summary of Couple Recommendations:

At the end of the face-to-face interviews each couple was asked, what advice would you give to couples considering marriage for the first time, or to couples on the journey of marriage? Following are some of their comments and advice:

Wife: "try to get along, sit around and talk things over is a must. Be in Christ, church is the foundation, stay involved with positive people; it is not easy."

Husband: "don't run to other people's house causing confusion."

Wife: "I think young couples need to understand that long-term marriages are not a cakewalk... Work at it, it's a job, be sincere and work at it be on one accord."

Husband: "must have trust, even if you're not a real religious person you must include God, you must do that,..."

Husband: "make up your mind that after the newness of marriage goes away you are going to work at it and bring it back. You have to be committed, first to your wife, the children, you need to be a father, and you need to be a husband. You make a lifetime commitment, when you say those vows, vows are serious stuff, if you are not 100% sure that you can make that commitment,…you need to think about whether or not to get married."

Wife: "be committed and be ready and willing to work at it when there's trouble, so seek counseling. I think that helped us through some of the hard times." "Some time you have to sit and think and count your blessings and don't sweat the small stuff." "Get away just the two of us; it was always with the kids except for a couple of special anniversaries, 20 and 25."

Wife: Communication.

Husband: "be able to receive rather than send, be able to listen and hear what the other person is saying and not always with your ears—non-verbal communication very important."

Wife: "go for it don't be selfish, make every moment count, make your time together special. Do not talk about each other to families, never put them down."

Husband: "make sure you share from the heart, let it be known how you feel, lay everything on the table."

Wife: "would not advise anybody to get married as young as I did, at 20. Think you need to mature, need to do some things as a young person before you become involved with someone else. Don't see how young people today, the way society is can make it if they get married that young."

Husband: "There is no road map, no puzzle pieces, it's trial and error, it's not by design, divine intervention, prayer, love, luck."

DISCUSSION

This study used the grounded theory approach to focus on two questions to examine the long-term African American marriage experiences: (1) Given the high rates of divorce in general and especially, among African American couples, what makes your marriage work and continue to endure successfully despite the statistics? (2) What are the challenges faced during the marital lifecycles? The literature review showed that historically, the African American family has been studied from a deficit oriented or deficiency-oriented model and not from a more contemporary view of strength. (As cited in Journal of Black Studies, 2000, by Billingsley, 1968, 1992, Gaines, 1997 Hill, 1972; McAdoo, 1992b; Mosley –Howard & Evans, 1995; Staples & Johnson, 1993). A number of issues and key themes emerged from the face-to-face interviews with the sample of diverse African American couples. These themes and the examples of some of their life experiences contribute to a better understanding of couple and family relationships, and challenges associated with an enduring and successful long-term marriage. Many of the key themes from this study are represented in the literature as characteristics of healthy couples. For example, research by Kaslow & Robison, 1996, identified commitment, communication, and religion/ spiritual as characteristics for healthy couples. Three of these themes also emerged from the current study. Other research showed similar responses to characteristics of successful marriages. Conversely, this current study identified two additional areas of importance, which were not necessarily found in previous research such as parental role models and education. Several couples mentioned the importance of completing their own education, and or making sure that their children were educated. From the examples by some of the couples in the study, persons went to extraordinary means and personal sacrifice to ensure that educational goals were attained.

The emphasis that several couples place on getting an education speaks to the value system of wanting to be prepared for whatever life experiences one may be faced with and the desire to be the best person they can be for themselves and for their families.

From an African American cultural perspective the emphasis on education as a key value to success including marital success in my opinion, stems from the Brown v. Board of Education of Topeka Kansas historic Supreme Court ruling. This historic ruling 50 years ago, declared *"separate educational facilities are inherently unequal.* This along with other civil rights movements and issues of the day remain engrained in the couples in this study who were raised during this time in history. For some of the couples they were the first in their families to graduate from high school and college and this reality allowed them to place a high valued on education for themselves and their children. These couples, even the ones who did not graduated high school knew the value of getting an education regardless of the choices they made, personally. A study about socioeconomic characteristics of middle-class black families indicates that one member of the marital couple almost always has attended college. The study further states that the husband and wife struggled and made great sacrifices to complete their formal education. As was exhibited by one of the couples in this study, college and graduate school are completed after adulthood and while the husband or wife, who also may be a parent, is employed fulltime. Also, it is noted according to one study that parents who experience struggles and hardships know that their status is directly correlated with their increased education (Willie, 1976).

In addition, research showed that long-term marriages highlighted characteristics such as appreciation, companionship, and sexual fidelity as important, Fennell 1987 as cited by Kaslow & Robison, 1996.) In this study, couples described intimacy as important and indicated a variety of ways to demonstrate intimacy, which can be interpreted within the definitions of previous research. This study found that nearly all of the couples reported having good intimate relationship with their husband or with their wife. Intimacy was described in a variety of ways, but all agreed that intimacy was important to the long-term success of their marriage. Some couples expressed that depending on what was happening in the marriage there may have been highs and lows of intimate expression, for example during times of stress when a couple was dealing with death, financial problems, and parenting issues.

Key to intimacy and marital success would be the removal of some stressors, in particular financial stress. At the time that the couples in this study were starting out as newly married, for example in the 1960s and 1970s, because of racial discrimination and income limitations of the kinds of jobs available to most African Americans it was necessary for both the husband and the wife to work. This has been historically the situation among African American marriages. For that reason, most husbands and wives act as partners out of necessity and have an equalitarian approach to the marriage, where neither husband nor wife has ultimate authority. African American husbands and wives work together to achieve a comfortable life style (Staples, 1986, p. 225). However, when one person in the marriage is the sole breadwinner, for example, the husband, the stress associated with striving to build a career, or maintain a technical trade as some couples in this study did; they were often at risk of experiencing economic hardship because of loss or the threat of loss of job, or career. This reality may have played a role in the level of intimacy and marital success. Research suggests that economic stress and its negative impact, for example, lack of employment, not having enough money to pay the bills are associated with depression, anxiety, low self-esteem, lower marital quality and authoritative parenting. (Conger et al., 1990; Elder, Conger, Foster, & Ardelt, 1992; McLoyd, 189, cited by Murry, McKenry & Price 2000, p.341).

The additional themes expressed by the husbands and wives in this study, communication, commitment, parental role models, religion/spirituality, and education provide insight and perspective into the myriad of differences and similarities that African American couples in long-term marriages face on a regular basis. It became obvious from the findings that many couples are faced with some difficult challenges as they pursue and endure the marital lifecycles. It was pointed out by one of the husbands that somehow the adversity they have endured has strengthened their marriage and brought them closer together. It is apparent that these couples have effective coping mechanisms to see them through the difficult circumstances.

Other factors contributing to the success of these marriages

When couples who have a long history of working outside the home, it was stated that having a spouse who helped with the housework was very much appreciated. Several husbands and wives share the housework including grocery shopping, lawn care, laundry, and childcare. The division of labor was shared equally among most of the couples when possible. African American women have historically been responsible for setting and crafting the various roles in the family. Role flexibility is expected from everyone in the household, including the husbands, and children especially when both parents work outside the home.

The majority of these couples handled conflict and problem solving by discussing their issues in ways that allowed both the husband the wife an opportunity to be heard. One or two of the couples would openly argue, but not in front of their children. All of the couples indicated that physical abuse was not used or tolerated within the marriage.

Theory Development

From the analysis, an overall finding was that these individuals and couples are highly involved and committed to their marriages. They all believe their marriages are successful not only based on the themes that emerged from the data and the experiences they had during the marital lifecycle but in my opinion, there is something more. Unique characteristics emerged from this sample, for example one of the wives dealt with the difficulty of her husband away in military service which often meant long periods of separation requiring role flexibility on the part of the couples. This wife was being a single parent to their infant child, and at the same time, completing her college degree, working and taking care of the home while her husband was in the Vietnam War. This couple as well as some of the others have demonstrated resiliency to hold on to each other and to maintain their families as best they could even under some extreme adversity. For example several of the couples have experienced very difficult parenting and grand parenting issues, major illness of a spouse, death of a child and, or beloved parents. In spite of these life challenges they responded to the difficult times in a manner that allowed them to grieve and heal to some extent in their own way and at the same time keep their marriages intact.

Another interesting discovery from the data analysis was the number of husbands who served in the military, in both the Korean War and the Vietnam War. Of the six husbands, two served in the Korean War and four served in the Vietnam War. This was a pivotal time in the history of this country and particularly for

African Americans as this was also the time when the Civil Rights Movement was at its peak. Major change was occurring in the nation at the time that many of these couples were starting their marriages and families. For this generation of African Americans there was a unique view of marriage compared with a more contemporary view. These couples faced racism within the social context of that time in history. There were social differences and perceptions that impacted wives whose husbands were dealing with the war experience.

Of interest also, was the number of husbands who had fathers in the home as they grew up during this historic time. Several of the husbands mentioned with pride the benefit of having a father that taught them how to be good husbands by role modeling good behavior with their mothers, as well as directly given them instructions on how to treat their wives.

While it was a time of change and growth, these families were dealing with life in the context of the larger society. For example they maneuvered through difficulty, fighting racism and segregation to complete their education, and for some who were likely first generation sons and daughters to attend college, and complete their degrees. Other participants were dealing with the employment situations at the time and possibly being some of the first African Americans hired in the companies they worked for which must have been challenging. In addition several of the couples mentioned the separation from their wives, and at least one child that was necessary during the times of war. This reality alone had to be extremely challenging for these young couples during that time. That period in our history is similar to the situation in our country today as many young couples are separated from loved ones, now because of the war in Iraq, for example.

While the analysis from the findings showed some similarities between the experiences of the some of the couples, clearly there were some differences as well. There were barriers that all the couples experienced but in spite of them, they were able to maintain healthy relationships with each other and with their children and grandchildren. Several of the couples indicated that their church involvement and their spirituality were key to sustaining them in times of trouble as well as being connected to a church family for support. Faith in God and having spirituality were conveyed by some participants who admitted they were not currently connected to a particular church; they were very connected with knowing that they have been very blessed. The literature review has found that in African American marriages that are successful that religion and spirituality are key factors. Diggs, & Pastor (1998). However, the divorce rate for those involved in church is about the same as for couples who are not in church. Obviously these couples have as the findings show many other characteristics that make for success in their marriages. These couples have demonstrated that marriage is a responsibility, an obligation and a lifelong commitment worth enduring in faith and in love.

The marital lifecycles of these couples also indicate a level of maturity, supportive extended family, and other resources in addition to pure determination. Given the young ages of all the couples at the point of marriage, the research would suggest these marriages would not last. The transition to parenthood has been shown to have an impact on marriages. Research suggests that when couples are in their twenties and become parents for the first time that these couples are more at risk for marital difficulty and likely divorce. Education levels and marriage expectations are also factors in the quality of the marriage at the time of becoming parents. The manner in which couples negotiate the demands of parenthood will determine the quality and strength of the marriage   (Helms-Erikson, 2001.)

Although the couples who are empty nesters appear to have found ways to transition to this stage of the marital lifecycle without too much difficult. Although one couple did express some disappointment with the level of intimacy or sexual activity, as a result of adult children and grandchildren returning home. This phenomena is established in the research as well, for example research indicates that couples who had launched their children, also known as empty nesters, viewed most aspects of their marriage positively except for sexual relationship (Mackey & O'Brien 1999).

In the study all except two couples have grandchildren. I thought it interesting how involved the grandfathers are with their grandchildren. Further research related to the importance of the grandparent role indicates that gender of the grandparent is important and that children report to have "warmer, more expressive relationships with grandmothers" (Eisenberg (988, p.205). Women typically are socialized toward maintaining family-based relationships which promotes the strongest ties between grandmothers and granddaughters. However, because male and female roles tend to shift after retirement, some researchers believe there is movement toward unisex gender roles for grandparents in how they relate to grandchildren (Spitz & Ward 1998). The research by Spitz & Ward suggest that the meaning of grandparenthood may be different for grandmothers and grandfathers.

Implications of the Study

The findings from this study lead to several implications for family life educators, social workers, church leaders and other professionals concerned about the African American marriage. Participants identified key themes of <u>communication</u>, <u>parental role</u> modeling, and <u>spirituality</u>, as the top reasons for the success of their marriages during the marital lifecycles.

Equally important is the high degree of resiliency demonstrated by participants in this study as well. Research on resiliency in African-American families shows that many of the themes identified by couples in this study are representative.

"Family resiliency is defined as the capacity to cultivate strengths to positively meet the challenges of life." (McCubbin, Hamilton; Thompson; Thompson; Futrell (1998.)

These couples having demonstrated the ability to adapt to most any situation put before them in the marriage. They have established roles, rules, goals and patterns of interactions that work for the marriage. Couples in this study have found that communication is very important to the marriage. One couple was clear about the value of non-verbal communication. Research by McCubbin et al. suggest that non-verbal interactions are more frequent and often more critical for relationship maintenance than verbal.

Spirituality and regular church attendance was instrumental in the marriages of most of the couples in this study. McCubbin (1998) indicates the family is really the context in which religious practice or cultural values are played out. Rituals and traditions gain meaning and emphasis in the context of family interaction and participation in the community. Religion and spirituality in the African American community play a key role in family life and raising children. The couples in this study are no exception. Spirituality is a central component in close personal relationships among individual members of the community. The roots of spirituality stem from the African, Caribbean, South American and Southern U. S. roots of most African Americans (McAdoo, 2003.) Because African American families tend to be multigenerational, the extended family support system is an on-going pattern in the family. The church family is an extension of the family consisting of non-relatives as well as blood relatives.

With this knowledge, individuals concerned with working with couples to strengthen marriages and families, could invest resources, and programs aimed at developing enhanced communication skills, coping skills for dealing with marital difficulties, and parenting challenges from pregnancy and child development through the adolescent years. Particular focus could be aimed at providing support to couples who are going through major illness such as cancer, as well as support for families who are grieving. Many African American families are stretched, and stressed, yet they are also resilient as these couples have demonstrated.

Strengths

One aspect of this study that was a strength was the couples themselves. These couples were very open with the researcher and all the couples appeared to enjoy the process. We all laughed a lot at some of the information as they shared. There were also some somber moments as some of the information they shared was sad, difficult and disappointing to them. I had the feeling that for several of the couples if not all, that this interview was the first opportunity the couples had to reflect on the journey of their marriage, and how much they had endured and enjoyed in a long time if ever. I found a richness in the deepness, and complexity of their stories.

Weaknesses

The participant sample size of six couples is relatively small. A larger participant sample perhaps from a broader geographical area could reveal even more insight to marital success in long-term married African American couples.

Conclusion

Future research aimed at transferability and further data analysis of what emerges from interviews with a larger sample may be beneficial. Also, additional theoretical frameworks, such as system theory, and exchange theory may provide even more specific knowledge of couple experiences. While in this study couples were interviewed together in their homes, consideration for interviewing the couple separately may provide a more in depth look at certain aspects of the marriage.

Given the divorce statistics and remarriage statistics in the general population and more specifically the African American population, additional study in this area could lend itself to supporting the creation of more marriages of strength and endurance for generations to come. There are many of married couples in our communities who are great role models. We don't often have the opportunity to have an in depth face to face discussion about the details and level of love and commitment involved in many African American marriages.

The role model that our **President Barack Obama and the First Lady Michelle Obama** demonstrate to the world of a healthy family and marriage, I believe, will be encouragement for all marriages, now and in the future.

CHALLENGE TO MY READERS

For those of you who are married, whether newly wed, been on the journey awhile, or planning/engaged to be married, answer the same interview questions where applicable, as the couples in this book, below:

INTERVIEW QUESTIONS

These interview questions are designed to be reflective in nature, and to give you an opportunity to recall significant aspects of your marriage.

1. What first attracted you to your spouse?

    _____

    _____

    _____

    _____

2. How did you meet?

    _____

    _____

    _____

    _____

    _____

3. Given the high divorce rate among African American couples today, what makes your marriage work?

    _____

    _____

    _____

4. Discuss the following:

Marriage and the joys and challenges of parenting (raising young children, adolescents, young adults)

_____

_____

_____

Children leaving home (empty nesters) _____

_____

_____

_____

_____

_____

Becoming grandparents_____

_____

_____

_____

_____

Marriage and Retirement_____

_____

_____

5. What have been the highlights, or best times of your marriage?

_____

_____

_____

_____

It is suggested that you review your responses periodically to capture what matters most in your marriage. Make updates as appropriate along the journey of your marriage, and share your experiences with your children, grandchildren and other youth, more importantly be a role model of a healthy and happy marriage.

Reference:

Arp, D. H, Arp, C. S., Stanley, S. M., Markman, H. J., Blumberg, S. L. (2000). Fighting for Your Empty Nest Marriage reinventing your relationship when the kids leave home. San Francisco, Jossey-Bass.

Barer, B. (2001). The 'Grands and Greats' of Very Old Black Grandmothers. Journal of Aging Studies, Vol. 15, Issue 1.

Burg, E. (2003). Community Marriage Initiatives: A New Vision for Building Stronger Marriages. National Council on Family Relations Report, Family Focus on Marriage, Volume 48:3, p. F6-F7.

Baydar, N., & Brooks-Gunn, J. (1998). Profiles of grandmothers who help care for their grandchildren in the United States. Family Relations, Vol. 47 p385-393.

Bryant, C. M. Conger, R. D., Meehan, J. m. (2001). Journal of Marriage & the Family, Vol. 63 Issue 3, p614.

Borgatti, S. (2004, March 22). Introduction to Grounded Theory, p. 1-5. Retrieved March 22, 2004, from http:www.analytictech.com/mb870/introtoGT.htm

Corbin, J., & Strauss, A. (1990). Grounded theory research: Procedures, canons, and evaluative criteria. Qualitative Sociology, 13, 3-21.

Cox, C. B. (2002). Empowering African American custodial grandparents. Social Work, Vol 47, p45-55.

Diggs, A. D. & Pastor, V. S. (1998). Staying married: a guide for African American couples. New York, NY: Kensington Publishing Co.

Edwards, K. J. (2003). It takes A Village To Save A Marriage. Journal of *Psychology and Theology*, Vol. 31, -188-196.

Eisenberg, A. R. (1988). Grandchildren's perspectives on relationship with grandparents: The influence of gender across generations. *Sex Roles*, 19, 205-217.

Fuller-Thomson, E. & Minkler, M. (2000). African American grandparents raising grandchildren: A national profile of demographic and health characteristics. Health & Social Work, Vol. 25, p109-119.

Glaser, B. G., & Strauss, A. L. (1967). The discovery of grounded theory. Chicago: Aldine.

Glen, N. D. (1998). The course of marital success and failure in five American 10-year marriage cohorts. *Journal of Marriage & the Family*, Vol. 60 Issue 3, p569.

Gottman, J., Silver, N. (1994). Why Marriages Succeed or Fail…and How You Can Make Yours Last. Simon & Schuster, New York.

Helms-Erikson, H. (2001). Marital Quality Ten Years After the Transition to Parenthood: Implications of the Timing of Parenthood and the Division of Housework. *Journal of Marriage & the Family*, Vol63 Issue 4, p1099.

Houck, J. W., & Daniel, R. W. (1994). Husbands' and wives' views of the communication in their marriages. *Journal of Humanistic Education & Development*, Vol. 33 Issue 1, p21.

Hurd, E. P. (1995). Quiet success: Parenting strengths among African Americans. *Families in Society*, Vol. 76 Issue 7, p434, 10p.

Kaslow, F. & Robison, J. A. (1996). Lon-Term Satisfying Marriages: Perceptions of Contributing Factors, The American Journal of Family Therapy, Vol 24, No. 2

King, V. (1997). The Legacy of Grandparenting: Childhood

experiences with grandparents and current involvement with grandchildren, *Journal of Marriage and the Family*, 59, 848-859.

Kinsel, B. I., (1983). <u>Thesis from start to finish: Marital Adjustment and Sex Role Orientation in Golden Wedding Anniversary Couples,</u> Miami University, Oxford, Ohio.

Landry, B., (2000). Black Working Wives, Pioneers of the American Family Revolution, Berkeley, University of California Press.

McAdoo, H. P. (1997). Black Families, third edition, SAGE Publications, Thousand Oaks

McAdoo, H. P. (2003). Religion in African American Families, National Council on Family Relations Report, Family Focus on Marriage, Volume 48:3, p. F10.

Mackey, R. A, & O'Brien, B. A. (1999). Adaptation in Lasting Marriages. <u>Families in Society</u>, 80, 587-596.

McCubbin, H. I., Thompson, E. A., Thompson, A. I., Futrell, J. A. (1998). Resiliency in African-American families. Sage Publications, Thousand Oaks, CA. Abstract retrieved April 13, 2004, from PsycINFO database.

McKenry, P. C., Price, S. J. (2000). Families & Change Coping with Stressful Events and Transitions, Sage Publications, Inc, p.346.

Mosley-Howard, G. S. & Evans, C. B. (2000), Relationships and Contemporary Experiences of The African American Family An Ethnographic Case Study. <u>Journal of Black Studies, Vol. 30 No. 3,</u> P.428-429).

Olson, D. H., & DeFrain,J. (1994). Marriage and the Family: Diversity and strength. Mountain View, CA: Mayfield Publishing Company.

Pinderhughes, E. B. (1978), Affliativeness in Western Nigeria social organization: Toward an understanding of modern, Black American lives (pp. 212-221).

The Ninth Congress of the National Association of Social

Workers, New York: National Association of Black Social Workers.

Pinderhughes, E. B. (1999). Black genealogy revisited: Restoring an African American family (pp. 19-199). In M. McGoldrick (ed.), Race, culture and gender in clinical practice, New York: Guilford Press.

Pinderhughes, E. B. (2002). African American Marriage in the 20th Century, Family Process, Vol. 41, No. 2, FPI, Inc. Pp. 269-282.

Querido, G. J., Warner, T. D., Eyberg, S. M. (2003). Parenting Styles and Child Behavior in African American Families of Preschool Children, *Journal of Clinical Child Psychology*, Vol. 31, No. 2, 272-277.

Robison, L. C. & Blanton, P. W. (1993). Marital strengths in enduring marriages, Family Relations: Vol. 42 issue 1, p38.

Sands, R. G., & Goldgerg-Glen, R. S. (2000). Factors associated with stress among grandparents raising their grandchildren. Family Relations, Vol. 49, p97-105.

Schoen, R., Astone, N. M., R, K., Standish, N. J. Kim, Y. J. (2002). Social Forces; Vol. 81 issue 2, p643.

Shirley, K. J. (2002). 'Resilient Marriages: From Alcoholism and Adversity to Relationship Growth. *Family Relations*; Vol. 51 Issue 2, p185

Staples, R. (1986). The Black Family: Essays and Studies. Socioeconomic Characteristics: The Black Family and Social Class, Charles V. Willie, (pp. 225-226). Wadsworth, Inc. Belmont, CA. 94002.

Strom, R. D., & Strom, S. K. (2000). Intergenerational learning and family harmony. Educational Gerontology, Vol. 26, p261-326.

Taylor, R. J., Chatters, L. M., Tucker, M. B., and Lewis, E. (1990). Developments in research on black families: a decade review. *Journal of Marriage and the Family*, 52(4), 993-1014.)

Watson, M. M., (2002). Thesis from start to finish: Exploration of the Views of Head Start Parents on the Effectiveness of the Head Start Program.

Whitfield, K. E., Markman, H. J., Standley, S. M., Blumberg,S. L. (2001). Fighting for Your African American Marriage. Jossey-Bass, A Wiley Company, San Francisco, CA

ABOUT THE AUTHOR

Annie Wimberly Rivers has been blessed to receive a Masters degree in Child and Family Studies, Miami University, Oxford, Ohio. She has been an instructor in Child Development in Diverse Families in the department of Family Studies at Miami. She grew up in the community of Lincoln Heights OH. She is an active member of Quinn Chapel A.M.E. Church, Forest Park OH. She is blessed to be the mother of two young adult daughters.